AF334957

SIGNIFYING PLACE

Signifying Place

The Semiotic Realisation of Place in Irish Product Marketing

SHEILA GAFFEY

ASHGATE

© Sheila Gaffey 2004

All rights reserved. No part of this publication may be reproduced, stored in a retrieval system, or transmitted in any form or by any means, electronic, mechanical, photocopying, recording or otherwise without the prior permission of the publisher.

Sheila Gaffey has asserted her right under the Copyright, Designs and Patents Act, 1988, to be identified as the author of this work.

Published by
Ashgate Publishing Limited
Gower House
Croft Road
Aldershot
Hants GU11 3HR
England

Ashgate Publishing Company
Suite 420
101 Cherry Street
Burlington, VT 05401-4405
USA

Ashgate website: http://www.ashgate.com

British Library Cataloguing in Publication Data
Gaffey, Sheila
Signifying place : the semiotic realisation of place in Irish product marketing
1. Geographical perception - Ireland 2. Regionalism - Ireland
3. Place marketing - Ireland 4. Handicrafts - Ireland - Marketing 5. Tourism - Ireland - Marketing 6. Ireland - Commerce
I. Title
304.2'3'09417

Library of Congress Cataloging-in-Publication Data
Gaffey, Sheila.
Signifying place : the semiotic realisation of place in Irish product marketing / Sheila Gaffey.
p. cm.
Based on the author's thesis (Ph. D.)--National University of Ireland, Galway, 2001.
Includes bibliographical references and index.
ISBN 0-7546-3934-7
1. Marketing--Ireland--Psychological aspects. 2. Advertising--Ireland--Psychological aspects. 3. Advertising--Tourism--Ireland--Psychological aspects. 4. Semiotics. I. Title.

HF5415.12.I73G34 2004
659.19'91417--dc22 2003062847

ISBN 0 7546 3934 7

Printed and bound in Great Britain by MPG Books Ltd, Bodmin, Cornwall

Contents

List of Figures

List of Tables

Preface

Regional images may be defined as representations of places which convey regional characteristics. International studies of the use of regional imagery relate primarily to place promotion for industry and tourism consumption, associations between product and place of production, and representations of rurality. Regional imagery has received some attention in the context of Ireland with reference to the evolution of such images in literature and tradition, particularly in the case of the West of Ireland, and their use for tourism promotion. However, few, if any, studies of the use of imagery in promotion at sub-national levels, or of individual products, have been undertaken. This work is an attempt to extend existing research on the use of regional imagery through highlighting the role of place (particularly, rural) imagery in the promotion of individual products and services in Ireland, identifying some of the critical issues concerning the development and application of these images, and analyzing some of the possible meanings which may be connotated through the use of such imagery. This book is based on work submitted and accepted for the degree of PhD at the National University of Ireland, Galway in 2001.

My PhD was partly based on research carried out for an EU funded research project under FAIR3-CT96-1827 on *Regional Imagery and the Promotion of Quality Products and Services in Lagging Regions of the EU* (RIPPLE). The objective of the project was to help public and private institutions develop strategies, policies and structures to aid the successful marketing and promotion of these quality products and services. As a Researcher on this project with a background in Communications Studies and Rural Development, my particular interest was in the use of imagery, especially images of place, by hand crafts and rural tourism small and medium sized enterprises (SMEs) in the promotion and marketing of their products. The RIPPLE project focused on two regions in Ireland: the Northwest and Southwest, and five categories of products and services: hand crafts, fish, organic produce, speciality foods and rural tourism. I decided to include a third study region, the Midlands, as an example of a lesser developed region, both in terms of the development of these particular industries and its perceived image in the public consciousness. I took part in the development of the RIPPLE questionnaires, including the conduct of extensive piloting and revision of draft formats, and I included extra questions relating to my area of interest whilst conducting the surveys. Data collected in both RIPPLE regions relating to hand crafts and rural tourism SMEs were utilized for the purposes of this present study, and additional research was carried out in the third study region. As well as developing a distinct conceptual framework, I conducted extensive analysis over and above that conducted for the RIPPLE project. This included a content classification and socio-semiotic analysis of promotional materials collected from respondents.

Acknowledgements

I wish to acknowledge the help and support of the following people:

Dr. Mary Cawley, Professor Ulf Strohmayer and Professor Brian Graham, for their assistance, encouragement, critiques and comments throughout the course of the work.

All of those who kindly gave of their time to participate in the surveys; without their assistance this research would not have been possible.

The RIPPLE project and research team for providing guidance, advice and support, in particular Professor Desmond Gillmor, Trinity College Dublin, the third member of the NUI, Galway laboratory, and Dr. Moya Kneafsey and Professor Brian Ilbery in the lead laboratory in Coventry University. The research team also included laboratories in France (University of Caen; CEMAGREF, Aubiére; ENITA, Clermont Ferrand), Finland (University of Helsinki), Greece (University of Patras), Ireland (Teagasc Rural Research Centre; Teagasc National Food Centre), Spain (University of Valencia), and the United Kingdom (Scottish Agricultural College, Aberdeen; University of Wales, Aberystwyth).

Dr. Mairead Corr and Marie Mahon for their useful comments and advice and Dr. Siubhán Comer for providing excellent maps, and for the use of her computer.

All of the staff and postgraduates of the Geography Department for their encouragement.

I owe personal thanks to my parents, John and Barbara Gaffey, and my family and friends for their unfailing support and encouragement in everything I do, and to Gerard and the O'Donovan family for their love and support.

Finally, I would like to acknowledge the support of the Irish Research Council for the Humanities and Social Sciences Postgraduate Scholarship 1999-2000 and Post-Doctoral Fellowship 2002-2003.

Galway, 2003 Sheila Gaffey

Chapter 1

Introduction

Regional images can be defined as 'representations, which in turn are understood as signs and symbols which are invested with particular meanings' (Ilbery and Kneafsey, 1997, p. 10). These images can consist of one or more of a variety of elements (e.g. people, animals, landscapes, including land, water and sky, folklore, legends) which are designed to convey regional characteristics. Burgess (1982) suggests that images of a place 'comprise an individual's beliefs, impressions, ideas and evaluations of different parts of the country' (p. 2) and can be created from a variety of different sources ranging from personal knowledge and experience to perceptions of environmental quality to preconceptions arising from stereotyped images used by the media. Research on the use of regional imagery has been carried out at different spatial levels and in a variety of contexts, ranging from place promotion of towns and cities to attract industrial investment, to representations of place for tourism consumption, to associations between product and place of production, to the changing representations of rurality (Bunce, 1994; Gold and Ward, 1994; Urry, 1995; Bell and Valentine, 1997; Hopkins, 1998). Haartsen *et al.* (2003) point out that representations of the rural can have practical impacts in numerous ways: influencing migration to rural areas; creating tourist expectations, and thus imposing commercialized representations on local populations (Brouwer, 1997); under-representing certain groups within these representations (Cloke and Little, 1997); and, influencing non-rural people's perceptions of rurality in terms of views on policy and decision making (Willits and Luloff, 1995). In fact, Rigg and Ritchie (2002) go so far as to state that 'when an imagined rurality comes into direct contact with the "real" rural the effects can be … deleterious for people striving to make a living in the countryside' (p. 370). Therefore, they conclude that 'the intersection of imagination with reality is both academically interesting and practically pertinent' (*ibid.*).

In relation to Ireland, the evolution of regional images in literature, tradition and Irish tourism promotion has received some attention, particularly in the case of the West of Ireland (Nash, 1993; Brett, 1994; Kiberd, 1995; Kneafsey, 1995; Kockel, 1995; Gibbons, 1996; Leerssen, 1996; Graham, 1997). Academic study of the use of regional images as marketing devices is of relatively recent origin and readily available studies relate in particular to links with the promotion of Ireland as a tourism destination (O'Connor, 1993; Quinn, B., 1994; Bell, 1995; Kneafsey, 1995; 1997). Few, if any, studies of the use of imagery in the promotion of sub-national levels have been undertaken. In addition, much of the research to date in this field has concentrated on the use of imagery to promote particular places, rather than products (Burgess, 1982; Burgess and Wood, 1988; Urry, 1990; Gold and Ward, 1994; Urry, 1995) and focused on the tourism sector (Hughes, 1992; O'Connor, 1993; Quinn, B., 1994; Mellinger, 1994; Bell, 1995; Hopkins, 1998) and urban spaces (Ashworth and Voogd, 1990; Duncan, 1990; Kearns and Philo, 1993; Dear and Flusty, 1999) in particular. The use of regional imagery in the promotion of individual tourism services has received less attention and its association with crafts is underexplored. I intend to address, to some degree, these gaps that exist in the literature through an analysis of the regional imagery used for the purposes of promotion and marketing by small producers of rural tourism and hand crafts products in Ireland and the organizations that support them.

History of Place Promotion

Place promotion, defined as 'the conscious use of publicity and marketing to communicate selective images of specific geographical localities or areas to a target audience', has a long history (Ward and Gold, 1994, p. 2). East coast American and Western European newspapers ran advertisements trying to tempt migrants to venture into new lands during the time of colonial development. These advertisements aimed to create appealing images of a fruitful and hospitable land and also to counteract negative images that already existed. From the mid 19th century there was a shift to encourage a more urban-based lifestyle. This became increasingly prevalent in the South of the U.S.A. after the Civil War in an effort to build a 'New South' based on industry and urbanization and was targeted mainly at northern investors (Ward, 1994). Also, in parts of Canada, particularly Ontario and Quebec, practical incentives were offered to attract industry. In Britain the only places being promoted in the 19th century were the new holiday resorts and were led by railway companies and local initiatives (Ward, 1998). This was due to the advanced industrialization and urbanization of the country in the early 19th century, so local authorities were more concerned with dealing with the attendant problems of industrialization than with trying to boost economic growth. When railways were introduced it was to an already established urban system. By 1900, new residential suburbs outside major cities were being promoted by developers and, again, railway companies. It was not until the 1930s that town promotion to attract industry became widespread. Since the 1960s locally-based place promotions have increased. Western de-industrialization has de-stabilized urban systems and place identities are changing as commercial, tourism and cultural promotion becomes widespread and not just the preserve of the traditional resorts. Ward and Gold (1994) argue that much of the imagery used has endured over the years, although updated to suit the times, and that even though more recent forms of place promotion such as out-of-town retail centres and large leisure complexes have introduced new themes, these images too have quickly become widespread and are recycled over and over again. This lack of creativity can be a result of inferior budgets for place promotion as compared to product-centred, major commercial campaigns, as well as poor professional practice. Also, specifically in relation to tourism,

> while the necessity for destinations to be imaginatively differentiated is recognised, in order to capture particular tourist markets, the process has been simultaneously criticised as a culturally homogenizing one (Hughes, 1998, p. 18).

Although place promotion is not a new phenomenon, it is only relatively recently that marketing approaches have been applied by public planning agencies as a philosophy of place management. New marketing concepts have evolved which have facilitated this development (Ashworth and Voogd, 1994). Marketing traditionally relates to selling physical products to paying customers whereas place marketing can be defined as

> a process whereby local activities are related as closely as possible to the demand of targeted customers ... to maximise the efficient social and economic functioning of the areas concerned, in accordance with whatever wider goals have been established (p. 41).

In this definition the concepts of *product*, *customer* and *marketing goals* differ greatly from standard marketing meanings. To address the problem of goals, the idea of *marketing in non-profit organizations* is useful (Ashworth and Voogd, 1990; 1994). Generally those involved in place marketing have goals which differ from those of private businesses, i.e. goals other than direct financial gain for those engaged in marketing. It is difficult to monitor the effectiveness of such marketing when there is no financial link between customer and business. Thus a different form of marketing which expands the notion of what makes up a market and includes the broader and longer-term goals of public authorities is necessary (Kotler and Zaltman, 1971 in Ashworth and Voogd, 1994).

Another new concept which has evolved is the idea of *social marketing* or what has become more accurately known as *attitudinal marketing*. This developed in the 1970s to accommodate the concern for longer term as well as immediate profits and also to influence aspects of customers' behaviour other than their purchasing activities. This often involved the pursuit of social goals which were usually seen as the responsibility of public authorities (Ashworth and Voogd, 1990). Thus, public authorities gained skills in marketing techniques. Also in the 1970s, the efficacy of *image marketing* became apparent, where images could be marketed even when the product was vague or even non-existent. This meant that places could be marketed with generalized images without having to define precisely the specific products that were being sold (Ashworth and Voogd, 1994). Ashworth and Voogd (1994) identify the importance of place images in place marketing. 'A place can only be commodified ... by means of a rigorous selection from its many characteristics. The results of this selection is the place-image' (p. 77).

Consumption Studies

Place promotion is generally examined in relation to public policy, marketing or image communication (Hopkins, 1998). This work looks primarily at the issue of image communication as part of promotional strategies, and as such it also contributes to the field of consumption studies in that it looks at aspects of what Sack (1988) has referred to as the 'language of consumption', i.e. advertising (p. 648).

The significant growth in attention being given to the topic of consumption by the academy in recent years is a 'delayed acknowledgement of social and economic transformations at a global level that had previously suffered from extraordinary academic neglect' (Miller, 1995, p. 1). This neglect is attributed to the dominance of the 'right' and 'left' political philosophies around which most modern ideas and beliefs gathered, defining themselves largely in opposition to each other, with small regard for real life. The means by which this ideological hegemony remained sheltered from reality was the elevation and advance of economics as an academic discipline, a discipline based on 'a system of other-worldly abstractions, providing a hermetic theory of ideal worlds of a purity rarely achieved in pre-secular religious beliefs' (p. 13). One such example of an abstract economic notion is its model of a rational consumer with no basis in actual social behaviour (Fine, 1995).

One form of consumption which is particularly relevant to the ways in which places are modelled, and has been neglected in academic research until recent years, is the consumption of tourism. Urry (1995) agrees that much of the writing to date about consumption assumes an asocial consumer and that no further 'work' is necessary after the purchase act. The tourist differs from the traditional model of a consumer in that tourism is mostly consumed by social groupings and there is a lot of 'work' involved by both holidaymakers and service providers in converting the various tourist services into a holiday experience. Another problem is that the actual services purchased do not necessarily make a good holiday experience, a lot depends on the particular social experience which cannot always be controlled. The fundamental characteristic of tourist activity is to look upon particular objects or landscapes which are different from the tourist's everyday experiences, so the actual purchases in tourism (the hotel, restaurant, airline tickets) are incidental to the gaze (Urry, 1990). The actual places are the objects of consumption, at least visually, which, in turn, has led to the commodification of places for tourists (Mitchell, 1998). Also in relation to the consumption of tourism, Urry (1995) discusses how travel and tourism have altered the modern and post-modern subject.

Changes in the social organization of travel and rapid forms of mobility have transformed the way in which people experience the modern world, 'changing both their forms of subjectivity and sociability and their aesthetic appreciation of nature, landscapes, townscapes and other societies' (p. 144). An important characteristic of modern society is the ability to monitor and evaluate itself, 'reflexive modernization'. Urry (1995) argues that such reflexivity can be aesthetic, with a 'proliferation of images and symbols operating at the level of feeling and consolidated around judgements of taste and distinction about different natures and different societies' (p. 145). Mobility and an ability to reflect upon other places and societies are central to this aesthetic reflexivity and become more important as issues such as culture, history and environment become more deeply embedded in the cultures of western society. The present appeal of heritage sites is a feature of aesthetic reflexivity (Urry, 1995).

Urry (1995) argues that with post-modernism we have seen the 'end of tourism' (p. 148). People are engaged in what might be called tourism practices much of the time, whether they are actually travelling or not, as they experience simulated mobility through the multiplicity and fluidity of signs and images which constantly surround them. In other words, it is no longer only when engaged in designated tourism practices that people purchase and consume visual signs and simulacra.

The huge growth in choice for consumers in all aspects of consumption has added to this explosion of images. This reflects what has been referred to as social and cultural de-differentiation (Lash, 1990), where there is a breakdown of the distinctiveness of different cultural spheres and the criteria governing them. Through the universal influence of the media and the 'aestheticization of everyday life', the purchase of images or visual consumption is becoming increasingly more pervasive in all aspects of society and the distinctions between '"high culture" and the "high street"' are breaking down (Urry, 1995, p. 149). Tourism has become 'de-differentiated' from other areas of interest, such as leisure, culture, shopping, education, hobbies and so on. Other aspects of "post-Fordist" consumption reflected in tourism include a growing rejection of certain types of mass tourism, increased market segmentation, the growth of alternative forms of tourism such as "green" tourism, and greater customization of holiday choices.

With post-modernism, the distinction between representations and reality has become blurred, 'since what we increasingly consume are signs or images: there is no simple "reality" separate from such modes of representation' (Urry, 1995, p. 149). Baudrillard takes this theory to its extreme in his vision of a world of simulacra (Poster, 1988). He argues that we now live in a hyperreality, where signs no longer have fixed referents; they are 'floating signifiers' (p. 4) referring to nothing other than themselves. De Certeau (1984) developed this position, arguing that 'the masses resignify meanings that are presented to them in the media, in consumer objects' (de Certeau, 1984 in Poster, 1988, p. 7). A body of research demonstrates this proposition, showing how the meanings of global products sometimes change in line with the values of the 'receiving' culture (Jackson, 1999). Such research comes within the remit of geographies of consumption.

Jackson and Thrift (1995) provide an overview of geographical research on consumption reviewing work on 'sites' of consumption (most notably focused on the gentrification of inner city areas, and shopping malls), the 'chains' linking locations of consumption (the most obvious work done in this area relates to the internationalization of food chains) and the 'spaces and places' of contemporary consumption. They argue that geographers have:

> injected a serious concern for space, place and the landscape into studies of advertising and the media and have been at the forefront of research on the production and consumption of environmental meanings, acknowledging our increasingly mediated understanding of the natural world (Jackson and Thrift, 1995, p. 228).

The use of spatial metaphors is widespread in consumption studies and Jackson and Thrift (1995) quote a particularly useful example, 'Lefebvre's distinction … between "spaces of representation" (such as shopping malls and department stores) and "representations of space" (in advertising and other media)' (Lefebvre, 1991 quoted in Jackson and Thrift, 1995, p. 218). Studies of the symbolic meanings of everyday spaces seek to unmask the numerous meanings that are hidden in contemporary consumption. Advertising is the 'dream world' of consumption and the conceptions and uses of spaces and places by advertisers affect those places (p. 223). Lagopoulos (1993) argues that the 'signifying aspects of space – the meaning of space for social subjects – are indeed equally as crucial to geography as the role of space in social processes' (p. 255). This work contributes to this project, as it is concerned with the 'representations of space', or place, and what these signify.

Although consumption has been 'duly "acknowledged" ' (Jackson, 1999, p. 95), existing geographical research on commodification has tended to concentrate on a narrow range of products (food and other retail products) and to look at commodification in a negative light, implying that 'once … cultures have been commodified, they have inevitably been devalued and degraded' (*ibid.*). The study of consumption must move beyond the morality of goods and, rather than aiming for an all-embracing definition of consumption, it is necessary to be aware of the diversity of contexts within which its meaning changes and to examine specific cases in depth (Miller, 1995). Jackson and Taylor (1996) and, more recently, Jackson (1999) also suggest that future research should move beyond the investigation of the commodification of particular kinds of manufactured products and services, to incorporate the study of the consumption of meanings in advertising, which may or may not lead to the consumption of the product itself. This book incorporates both propositions in that it examines in depth the particular 'languages of consumption' used in specific cases, i.e. to commodify rural tourism and hand crafts in three regions in Ireland.

The Study Regions

The study regions are located in three geographically distinctive contexts in the Midlands, Northwest and Southwest of Ireland (Figure 1.1). The Midlands region comprises counties Laois, Offaly and Westmeath. The Northwest, as defined for study purposes, combines counties Leitrim, Roscommon and Sligo. The Southwest study region comprises county Kerry and the western part of county Cork (including Bandon, Bantry, Castletown, Clonakilty, Dunmanway, Kinsale,

Skibbereen and Skull Rural Districts, and Clonakilty, Kinsale and Skibbereen Urban Districts).

Figure 1.1 Location of study regions within the Republic of Ireland

The three study regions provide contrasts in terms of topography, demography, economy, market opportunities and in the extent to which they have an established "image" in the public consciousness. The Southwest has a larger and more prosperous economy, both in terms of farming and non-farming activities. The southern and south-western areas have a well-developed tourist infrastructure, with regard to accommodation provision and recreational activities, and the region is well known as a tourist destination. Tourism is less well established in the Northwest, but the region, and particularly county Sligo, is developing a reputation as a holiday destination for those who wish to get off the beaten path. Traditionally, the Midlands has not been viewed as a holiday destination and the accommodation and activity infrastructure has been underdeveloped. There is, however, a recognized reputation for coarse angling and a growing one for cruising on the Shannon and Grand Canal. Hand crafts are well-established in the Southwest and are of growing importance in the Northwest, particularly among in-migrants. However, professional craftworkers are uncommon in the Midlands and the region is not usually associated with arts and hand crafts. All three regions have been identified in Irish and European Union policy measures as being characterized by below average national and EU levels of economic and social development (Copus, 1996; Government of Ireland, 1999).

The three study regions also provide contrasts in terms of the types of regional images that exist and differ also in the extent to which place images have been developed and utilized in the promotion and marketing of regional products and services. The Southwest is best developed in this regard, with place images such as Bantry Bay, the Lakes of Killarney, the Ring of Kerry and the rugged mountain and Atlantic coastal scenery being internationally recognized and utilized in promoting not only the region, but the country as a whole. West Cork has developed a reputation for artisan food production, particularly farmhouse cheeses which use place names as marketing devices. While the image of the Northwest region is less well developed, the landscape of Sligo in particular has a certain reputation arising from the writings of W. B. Yeats. This has been exploited in the establishment of the 'Yeats Country' characterization, which is utilized by disparate businesses in the county. More recently, local development organizations have attempted to establish county brands for the promotion of regional crafts and tourism. The Midlands is least well-known, being traditionally identified as 'flat' and as a place to pass through on the way to the West of the country. Local agencies in this region are least active in developing promotional strategies to combat these negative images.

The Products and Services

Each region provides examples of a number of quality rural tourism and hand crafts producers, many of whom are currently using regional imagery in varying ways and to different degrees in promoting their products and services, either in naming or branding their product or in promotional literature. Producers and providers of these selected products and services are often more inclined to use regional imagery in promotion and marketing than other producers, for a number of reasons. Tourism providers use regional imagery to sell a place as well as a product and, by their nature, tourism products often incorporate aspects of place, e.g. golf courses, heritage attractions and angling and cruising facilities. Many hand crafts producers use their environment as inspiration in designing their products, and some use local raw materials in production. In many areas, indigenous crafts are part of the tourism product and producers attempt to tap into the tourist market through utilizing regional imagery in their promotion. Also, in general, 'quality' producers may be more likely to use regional imagery than others, because of the niche values attached to associating with a particular place, as I will discuss in Chapter 7.

Analysis and Results

A number of distinct research tasks were carried out throughout the course of this study. These included identifying the images of the three study regions held by producers and organizations, determining the methods employed to utilize links to place and regional imagery in the promotion of crafts and rural tourism, categorizing and analyzing the content of producers' promotional materials and selecting case studies which best illustrate the various ways in which regional imagery was utilized in promotion. The results of these research tasks are presented in the following pages. In this way, I aim to highlight the role of place (particularly, rural) imagery in the promotion of individual products and services in Ireland, stress some of the critical issues concerning the development and application of these images, and suggest some of the possible meanings which may be connotated through the use of such imagery.

The method employed to analyze the imagery used by producers involved conducting a content analysis and socio-semiotic investigation of their promotional materials in order to identify the ideologies and myths connoted by these images. In Chapter 2, I outline the specific techniques which comprise this method of analysis as it was applied in this case. Chapter 3 describes the results of the quantitative analysis of the content of the promotional materials. The results of this analysis are discussed in Chapters 4 to 8 in the context of a number of themes identified in the literature pertaining to this topic. In Chapter 4, I consider the ways in which Western society has developed particular 'ways of seeing' rurality, countryside and landscape and examine how the promotional materials analyzed tap into and support these socially constructed meanings. Chapter 5 examines the symbolic meanings of place in promotion and it is demonstrated that myths develop which mark certain objects and areas as being 'sight worthy' and that tourism, especially, but not exclusively, constructs people's views of particular places. Once a place becomes 'sight worthy', it must be promoted as such, so places are increasingly commodified for this purpose. As part of the commodification process, existing images (real and mythical) of places are adapted and utilized. This can result in a very limited/stereotyped image of a place being promoted, as is demonstrated in Chapter 6 in relation to the dissemination of real and imagined images of the landscape of the West of Ireland, and in the promotion of rural areas, generally, and Ireland, specifically, as a tourist destination. Chapter 7 examines the role of place imagery in the production of 'uniqueness', and highlights the ways in which images which symbolize regional distinctiveness can be used as a method of product differentiation, especially when this distinctiveness is equated with quality and authenticity. The role of place myths in the creation of social spaces is considered in Chapter 8, particularly in relation to tourism. It is increasingly recognized that tourism promotional bodies contribute greatly to the creation of the imagined geographies of places abroad through place representation. However, arguments have been made for the continuation of particular place images, where economic benefits can be identified. Finally, Chapter 9 concludes with a review of the findings of the research in the context of a number of interrelated themes, namely: the processes involved in place image creation and promotion; the actual imagery used and meanings signified; and some of the implications of these findings.

Chapter 2

Semiotics and Other Methodological Issues

In the late 1960s, there was a reaction against quantitative methods within human geography. Some argued that 'geography as the study of spatial relationships was an incomplete and unsatisfactory view of the discipline, telling only part of a complex story' and that many research problems were not amenable to quantitative analysis which required large samples and standard statistical tests (Robinson, 1998, p. 407-8). A range of new methods has been utilized by geographers in the last two decades including qualitative and interpretive techniques traditionally associated with anthropology and sociology, although having currency in humanistic studies in geography (Buttimer and Seamon, 1980). These methods normally work on the basis that reality is viewed and understood in different ways by different groups and individuals, and the analysis of meanings in specific contexts is usually emphasized rather than the expression of generalities.

Qualitative techniques are often used to supplement statistical surveys and quantitative analysis, to attain a more complete description of the research topic (Mason, 1994). Qualitative data can take a great variety of forms. Text, art, design and visual images can all communicate qualitative information. The nature of qualitative research is to employ a variety of interconnected methods in order to develop an in-depth understanding of the subject at hand. Denzin and Lincoln (1994) discuss this type of research as a bricolage and the researcher as *bricoleur*. A bricolage is 'a pieced-together, close-knit set of practices that provide solutions to a problem in a concrete situation' (p. 2). The bricoleur is a 'Jack of all trades or a kind of professional do-it-yourself person' (Lévi-Strauss, 1966 quoted in Denzin and Lincoln, 1994, p. 2) who utilizes whatever methodological strategies and tools are necessary, depending on the research questions and the context. If existing tools are insufficient, the bricoleur will invent or piece together new tools. Walker (1985a) agrees that the analysis of qualitative data must be 'explicitly interpretive, creative and personal ... [but] systematic and careful' (p. 3).

Robinson (1998) identifies four broad categories of qualitative techniques which are most commonly used by geographers:

1. Questionnaire survey methods (formal interviews)
2. Non-directional interviews or informal surveys
3. Participant observation
4. Interpretation of "supporting" documentation and "texts", e.g. plans, paintings, newspapers, advertising (p. 11).

The study upon which this book is based used techniques which fall under categories 1 and 4. Two separate questionnaire surveys were carried out: the first involved a survey of businesses involved in the production of crafts products and tourism services; and the second comprised a survey of support organizations. The producers interviewed in the three regions did not constitute a random sample; they were selected for interview purposively. Purposeful sampling as a strategy allows for the deliberate selection of 'people with specific characteristics, behaviour or experience which may be postulated to offer different perspectives on the research problem' (Walker, 1985b, p. 179). The advantage of such a sampling strategy includes achieving representativeness of the settings, individuals or activities selected, as well as capturing the heterogeneity of the population. Purposeful sampling also allows for specific investigation of cases which are critical for the study thesis and can be used to provide comparisons to illustrate reasons for differences between cases (Maxwell, 1998). In the current study, all producer enterprises were (i) SMEs, employing 50 full-time employees or less, and (ii) producers of quality hand crafts and rural tourism products and services. The products and services were selected with reference to a series of quality criteria, which included: (i) certification, i.e. self-regulation or possession of a quality mark/symbol; (ii) association, i.e. regional designation or local environment/cultural/historical connection; (iii) specification, i.e. production/service method, raw materials; (iv) attraction, i.e. tapping into subliminal wants of consumers in terms of design, texture, appearance, premium price, personal attention (for a fuller explanation of criteria see Ilbery and Kneafsey, 2000). The products and services represented were hand crafts (including fine art products, such as paintings and sculptures) and rural tourism (including accommodation and recreational activities) (Table 2.1). Whilst some products and services were common to both regions, region-specific products were included also.

Table 2.1 Selected products and services

MIDLANDS	NORTHWEST	SOUTHWEST
Hand crafts (n=10)	**Hand crafts (n=20)**	**Hand crafts (n=22)**
Handmade craft products (wood work, bronze, pewter, textiles)	Handmade craft products (textiles, pottery, leather-goods, jewellery)	Handmade craft products (textiles, pottery, leather-goods, jewellery)
Fine art products	Fine art products	Fine art products
Rural tourism (n=30)	**Rural tourism (n=28)**	**Rural tourism (n=29)**
Quality accommodation	Quality accommodation	Quality accommodation
Angling	Angling	Angling
Cabin cruising	Cabin cruising	Golf clubs
Golf clubs	Golf clubs	Heritage attractions
Heritage attractions	Heritage attractions	Recreational activities
Open farms	Open farms	
Recreational activities	Recreational activities	

As with the producer survey, the organizations interviewed did not constitute a random sample; they were selected for interview purposively based on the information provided by the producers, desk research conducted into the relevant sectors, and consultation with sectoral experts. The organizations surveyed ranged from national sectoral agencies whose sole remit was the development and/or marketing of tourism or crafts only, to regional and local multi-sectoral economic development bodies such as LEADER[1] companies and County Enterprise Boards.[2] The data from the surveys was supplemented by supporting documentation, in the form of policy papers, evaluation reports and information documents, in the case of the organizational survey, and promotional materials, in the case of both surveys. Analysis and interpretation of this data involved a combination of quantitative and qualitative methods, ranging from a statistical analysis, using the Statistical Package for the Social Sciences (SPSS), of the closed questions used in the questionnaire surveys to a highly subjective interpretative deconstruction, rooted in socio-semiotic analysis, of the text and images communicated in producers' promotional materials.

Three different emphases in the study of promotional messages as image communication may be identified: the action of image production and communication; the message of the media, both manifest and latent meanings; and, audience decoding of media messages – in other words, the sender, the message and the receiver. This research concentrates on the message and a number of different approaches to its study exist. Art historical approaches using picture analysis to examine visual elements of promotional materials such as posters can be used, but certain emphases within the approach mitigate against its use in the study of promotional materials. The methodology promotes investigation of the association between the symbolism of images and artistic movements and techniques, as well as the general development of the individual artist's work in place representation. However, most place promotional material is anonymous. The second set of approaches to examining message content developed from cognitive-behaviouralism and looks at the role of stereotypes and how place images are perceived. However, its emphasis on the individual and the role of mental imagery overlooks the cultural context of the image communication process which is an important element in understanding the complete meaning of media messages (Gold, 1994). The third approach, and one which was used in the present research, is content analysis.

Simply put, content analysis is a research method for analyzing the content of documents. It arose out of social scientific approaches to mass communication research and is used by most researchers of media messages. Content analysis 'allows us to understand the form and substance of messages, and the choices made by speakers and writers … to discern the strategies of messengers, compare different types of messages' (Schrott and Lanoue, 1994, p. 327).

Krippendorff (1980) defines content analysis as 'a research technique for making replicative and valid inferences from data to their context' (p. 21). This emphasis on the relationship between the content of texts and their institutional, societal and cultural contexts is important (Schrott and Lanoue, 1994). Traditional quantitative methods such as frequency counts and key word analysis have been joined by more qualitative approaches which seek to determine the latent messages in communicated materials, although studies on the content of place promotional materials are still limited (Gold, 1994). This study seeks to add to this literature. An advantage of content analysis is that both quantitative and qualitative methods can be used to analyze texts. Quantification is useful in that it allows for more accurate comparisons between different texts, it identifies how much more (or less) attention is given to some topics than to others, and, it often exposes similarities and differences between texts that would be difficult to detect otherwise (Weber, 1994). Content analysis can be used to analyze any "text", whether it takes the form of writing, sound or pictures. Whatever the text, the analysis generally adheres to a basic procedure, as follows (Denscombe, 1998).

1. **Firstly, an appropriate sample of text is chosen.** In this case, the sample was 253 pieces of promotional material used by the selected producers. This did not constitute the entire range of materials used by these producers; it was the promotional literature provided by the respondents on the day of the interview. Not every respondent had an example of any or all of their literature on the given day.
2. **The next step involves breaking the text down into smaller component units for analysis.** In this case, the texts were composed of words, photographs, sketches, slogans, logos and approval symbols and each of these units was analyzed separately.
3. **Suitable categories must be developed for analyzing the data.** These are issues with which the researcher is concerned and which may occur in the text in different forms. For example, in relation to the present study, the issue of relevance was the use of regional imagery in promotional materials. Categories of meaning were gleaned from the promotional materials themselves. Guetzkow (1950) suggests that 150 units of analysis are sufficient to develop a coding guide, so a sample of 60 different pieces of promotional literature was selected, most containing three or more different units of analysis. Eleven categories were identified and the remaining texts were analyzed accordingly.
4. **The next step involves coding the units in line with the categories.** In this case, this simply involved writing the pertinent code on the actual text.
5. **The frequency with which each of the units occurs is now counted.** For this study, a frequency table was compiled which summarized the occurrence of each category within each unit of analysis.

To summarize, an analysis of 253 pieces of promotional literature used by the selected producers was carried out in order to understand the content, or 'form and substance' (Schrott and Lanoue, 1994, p. 327), of these messages to potential consumers. This content analysis provided an overview of the signifiers (the physical existence of the sign) used in this particular sign system. A quantitative assessment indicated the medium and format of the place promotional messages and the different elements of the format provided the smaller component units used for additional analysis. Categories were developed for analyzing the data further and each unit of analysis was assigned a category. These categories were the subject of a socio-semiotic analysis, albeit a simplified one, to identify the ideologies and myths connoted by these promotional materials.

Traditional methods of simply quantifying the content of texts tend to dislocate the units and their meaning from their context. It is also difficult for this type of analysis to deal with content in terms of its implied meanings. A combination of qualitative hermeneutic approaches with the traditional quantitative approach described above may be utilized to overcome this problem (Schrott and Lanoue, 1994). Interpretive methods may be used to ascertain the meaning of each unit of text which may then be categorized and coded for quantitative analysis. A meticulous interpretation of any text must use, implicitly or explicitly, the five principles or canons of hermeneutic analysis (Pickles, 1992): (i) meaning must be derived from, and not projected into, the text; (ii) the interpreter's evaluation must be rooted in the text itself, its forms, conventions and assertions; (iii) the interpreter must show the meaning the text had for its intended readers and the meaning it has today within the framework of modern perceptions, concerns and biases; (iv) the 'hermeneutic circle' (p. 225) must be observed, in other words, the whole can only be understood in relation to its parts and the parts can only be understood in relation to the whole; and, (v) the interpreter must make appropriate suppositions in order to make explicit details which the author and/or readers left implicit. This present study combined a qualitative hermeneutic approach, which implicitly employed these principles of hermeneutic analysis, with a traditional quantitative content analysis in the investigation of the textual elements of the promotional literature.

Having identified the content of the promotional materials, an analytical method derived from a theoretical approach anchored in the field of cultural studies, namely structuralism, was used to interpret the meanings of the texts. Structuralism

> sees language as the fundamental structure of social life determining the signifying practices of different cultures... [it] is concerned not only with conventional verbal languages but also any sign-system which has language-like properties (Gold, 1994, p. 27).

Structuralist approaches often use semiotic analysis and look less to the sign-system itself than to the meaning of particular texts in their cultural context.

It is useful here to outline some basic concepts of semiotics or the study of signs (Nöth, 1995). The Swiss linguist, Ferdinand de Saussure (1974), was one of the founders of semiotics and, although primarily interested in language, his model of elements of meaning is a useful starting point in the study of signs in general, including promotional materials (Blonsky, 1985). For Saussure, the sign consisted of a *signifier* and a *signified*, for analytical purposes only. The signifier is the physical existence of the sign as we perceive it, in other words the marks on the paper (e.g. FLOWER). The signified is the mental concept to which the signifier refers (in this case our mental image of a plant with a green stem and colourful petals). The relationship between the signifier and the signified brings about the meaning or *signification* (Fiske, 1990). A sign system is 'a systematically related collection of objects, events or phenomena taken as signs, such as the words comprising this sentence and the meanings and ideas it conveys' (Hopkins, 1998, p. 68). Semiotics is not only used in the study of language, but can be applied to all sign systems. As signification is about the production and consumption of signs, then all aspects of culture can potentially be subject to semiotic analysis (Eco, 1976).

Saussure observed that there is no logical link between the signifier and signified, the relationship is purely arbitrary, 'fixed for a certain time by the nuances of political culture' (Aitken, 1997, p. 205). In order to read signs, people must learn a set of codes for different kinds of texts. People are not generally conscious of this process, part of being socialized into a culture is being taught the codes of that culture. Semiotics is about consciously deciphering these codes. A discussion of a number of concepts of semiotics follows, all of which will be referred to in the socio-semiotic analysis of the promotional literature.

The philosopher and logician, Charles Sanders Pierce (1931-58), divided signs into three types: *icon*, *index* and *symbol*. An iconic sign resembles its object, e.g. photographs. In an index there is a direct link between the sign and its object, e.g. smoke is an index of a fire. With the third type of sign, the symbol, there is no resemblance or direct link between the sign and the object, the connection is purely arbitrary, e.g. numbers and written words (Nöth, 1995).

As already mentioned, Saussure was primarily interested in the linguistic system of signs and how language related to the reality to which it referred. He had little interest in how signs related to the reader. In other words, he concentrated on the text, not the way in which the signs interacted with the personal and cultural experiences of the reader. A follower of Saussure's, Roland Barthes, developed a theory for analyzing this interactive idea of meaning. Barthes saw two *orders of signification*. The first, *denotation*, refers to the obvious meaning of a sign, e.g. a photograph of a house denotes that particular house.

In the second order of signification, signs work in three ways. *Connotation*, the first of the three ways, describes the way in which meanings become more subjective, the meaning is interpreted by the reader in terms of his/her own beliefs, feelings and culture. Barthes (1977) uses the example of photography to illustrate the difference between denotation and connotation. Denotation is the actual, mechanical reproduction of the object at which the camera is pointed. Connotation relates to how the object is photographed, the film, frame, angle, focus and background that are used. These elements can connote different meanings.

The second of the three ways in which signs work in the second order is through what Barthes (1973) called *myth*. Barthes saw a myth as a culture's way of thinking about or understanding some aspect of reality or nature. So a sign that connotes a particular image, e.g. a man and woman standing in front of the Eiffel Tower in Paris, which connotes feelings of romance and love, relies for its meaning on the fact that the myth of Paris as a city of romance is common in our culture.

The third way of signifying in this second order is through *symbols*. Symbols are created through conventional use of a particular object to stand for something else. For example, a white dove with an olive branch symbolizes peace. This is similar to Pierce's term, symbol, as discussed above.

Three other concepts which are widely used to describe aspects of semiotics are *intertextuality*, *metaphor* and *metonymy*. These ideas characterize the basic way that messages accomplish their referential role (Jakobson and Halle, 1956). Intertextuality indicates 'the conscious or unconscious use of previously created texts' (Aitken, 1997, p. 205). In order to completely understand the newly created text, readers must be aware of the original text. Intertextuality is frequently used in cinema, either as a parody (as in the *Naked Gun* series (1988-1994) and many of the comedy director, Mel Brookes' (1926-), films) or as a *homage* to another film director's work (e.g. the famous *Battleship Potemkin* (Sergei Eisenstein, 1925) inspired shoot-out on the train station steps in Brian de Palma's (1987) *The Untouchables*). More self-conscious forms of intertextuality, such as film "remakes" or the numerous references to the media in the animated cartoon *The Simpsons* (1987-), credit the audience 'with the necessary experience to make sense of such allusions and offers them the pleasure of recognition ... it appeals to the pleasures of critical detachment rather than of emotional involvement' (Chandler, 2000, p. 3). For the reader to fully appreciate the conveyed message, a knowledge, or perhaps only a recognition, of the referenced texts is desirable.

A metaphor expresses 'the unfamiliar in terms of the familiar' (Fiske, 1990, p. 92), e.g. the barbarian hordes *mowed down* the villagers (the mowing is familiar, the barbarians' actions are not). Outside literary tradition, metaphors are used in visual language by advertisers, e.g. the man on the surf board, the waves and the surf were a metaphor for a well known Irish stout.

Metonymy works by making a part of reality stand for the whole, in other words they work indexically, e.g. smoke indicates fire. Metonyms purport to represent reality, to be natural, because of this indexical link. This can be misleading in that the part shown is not the whole reality. For example, out of a large photograph of one hundred people attending a conference, a small frame showing one person who has fallen asleep could be published in a newspaper purporting to represent the mood of the conference: long and tedious. Fiske (1990) points out that 'myths work metonymically in that one sign ... stimulates us to construct the rest of the chain of concepts that constitute a myth' (p. 96).

One aspect of Saussure's work on semiotics was that a sign's meaning was largely determined by its relationship to other signs and the two main types of relationships were *paradigmatic* and *syntagmatic* (Fiske, 1990). The paradigm is the set of signs from which the choice is made (e.g. the number 7 is a member of the numeric paradigm) and only one item from that set can be chosen. Communication involves making a choice, selecting from a paradigm, and the meaning of the selection is largely determined by the meaning of the items not chosen. The syntagm is the combination of the item chosen with other signs, e.g. a word is a paradigmatic choice from a set of possible words and a sentence is a syntagm of words. An important aspect of syntagms is that they are governed by rules or conventions, e.g. sentences are governed by grammar. The structural anthropologist, Lévi-Strauss, extended Saussure's theory of language as a structural system to cover all cultural systems and he believed the paradigmatic dimension of language was the most important, particularly the notion of *binary oppositions* (*ibid.*). This is the notion that everything falls into either category A or B and that neither can exist on their own, they only make sense in relation to each other. Something belongs to category A because it does not belong to category B, e.g. light and dark, earth and air, man and woman. Of course, in reality, there are shades of grey, what Lévi-Strauss called *anomalous categories* or categories that partake of characteristics of both the binarily opposed ones.

Other approaches to the interpretation of meanings permit more varied readings than structuralist interpretations. A range of new research methods has arisen, including 'cultural critique, deconstruction, new linguistic theory, cultural hermeneutics, post-colonial theory and various brands of post-structural and post-modern analysis' (Gold, 1994, p. 28). These help move comprehension of message content beyond the restrictions of the other approaches described and consider the ideological and rhetorical meanings of messages. Gold (1994) defines *ideology* as the 'pervasive set of ideas, beliefs and images that groups employ to make the world more intelligible… an essential part of the process by which people come to terms with the world around them' (p. 28).

This is similar to Barthes' definition of *myths*. The meaning of promotional messages is therefore created and negotiated within the wider ideological context. Ideology habitually leads to conformity, with promotional materials becoming increasingly homogenous as they use the same types of imagery and language, because producers and consumers of images share comparable ideological perspectives. This 'set of shared needs and understandings could be said to contribute to the similarities in the resulting rhetoric' (Gold, 1994, p. 29).

Rhetoric is defined as 'the use of discourse… to inform or persuade or move an audience' (Corbett, 1971 quoted in Gold, 1994, p. 29). It requires that the audience feels the sender of the message is credible and that the sender has a sound awareness of the audience and their needs. Gold (1994) gives several examples of rhetorical methods by which images are created and manifested in their cultural contexts: industrial place promotion is directed almost entirely at men, and women seldom appear in promotional materials; puns are used to attract readers' attentions and imply a humorous exchange between equals (advertisers need an accurate knowledge of their audience for this to work effectively); slogans are used to communicate key points in a short and simple manner; advertisers attempt to give credibility to their dialogue by referring to former accomplishments in attracting migrants or by quoting independent "experts" who give favourable opinions about the place; transport is believed to be important in locational terms so road network links and maps are used to profess centrality; symbols of nature are increasingly important in terms of their value in Western society and also to convey abstract ideas such as "growth"; terminology related to enterprise, lifestyle and culture are also increasingly used in the rhetorical discourse of place promotion.

Structuralism and semiotics have been criticized for placing too much emphasis on the text and not enough on the reader and their social situation (Eco,

1976; Deleuze, 1988). Socio-semiotics is a branch of semiotics which seeks to address this by examining both signs and their social context (Gottdiener, 1995). As demonstrated, sign systems are ideologically negotiated and socio-semiotics looks at 'the junction of the signifiers of the sign ... and the signified ideologies of the sign' (Hopkins, 1998, p. 68). In other words it examines the link between the material culture of everyday life and the sign system (Gottdiener, 1995). For socio-semiotics, all meaning arises from the connotative meaning of the sign.

> Both the produced object world itself and our understanding of it derives from codified ideologies that are aspects of social practice and their socialization processes. The latter articulation constitutes the object of analysis for socio-semiotics (p. 26).

In the case of this study, the aspects of material culture examined were place promotional materials used by specified producers. The analysis involved identifying and interpreting the myths and ideologies connoted by the text and images in these materials within the context of the culture in which these meanings were produced and consumed.

Having conducted a content analysis of the promotional materials as a whole, case studies were selected which best illustrated some of the themes identified. The case study is not so much a method of research as a strategy. It aims to understand one case in detail, acknowledging its complexity and its circumstances, using whatever methods are deemed suitable (Punch, 1998). The utilization of a diversity of evidence has been highlighted as an important element in case study research (Yin, 1998). As an analytical strategy, case studies are examples of non-cross-sectional data organization (Mason, 1996). Much qualitative data is subject to cross-sectional organization, whereby the same set of indexing categories are used across the whole data set. This was the case in the overall analysis of the producer and organizational surveys, where the analytical logic was to compare cross-sectionally parts or themes of each of the units of data, i.e. the questionnaires. In contrast, non-cross-sectional data organization involves 'looking at discrete parts, bits or units within your data set, and documenting something about those parts specifically' (p. 128). It is not necessary to have begun your study as "case study research" to be able to identify case studies within the data set for analytic purposes, in this instance, selected individual producers. The relevance of case study examination is 'to validate deductions by reference to specific social episodes ... [and] also facilitates the presentation of different kinds of data' (Bastin, 1985, p. 99).

In the current study, *instrumental case studies* were selected for in-depth analysis, where 'a particular case is examined to provide insight into an issue ... The case is of secondary interest; it plays a supportive role, facilitating our understanding of something else' (Stake, 1994, p. 237). The cases were selected to illustrate the best examples from the data set of the use of place imagery as a promotion and marketing strategy by small-scale crafts and tourism businesses. The overall analysis of the producer and organizational surveys, together with the content analysis of producers' promotional materials, highlighted the various ways in which regional imagery was utilized in general in promotion. Cases were selected which best illustrated these points.

So, to recap, content analysis was used to identify the signifiers used in this particular sign system. These signifiers were subject to a quantitative evaluation which allowed categories to be developed which sorted the different elements of the signs into smaller component units for further investigation. A simple socio-semiotic analysis of these categories, with a particular emphasis on logos, slogans, photographs and text, highlights some of the ideologies and myths connoted by the promotional materials, and it is with this analysis that the remainder of the book is primarily concerned.

Notes

1 LEADER (*Liaison entre action de Développement de l'Economie Rurale*/ links between actions for the development of the rural economy) is a Community Programme for Rural Development in rural regions aimed at local development agencies having an integrated rural development strategy, involving partners from public, private and voluntary sectors.

2 There are 35 State and EU funded City/County Enterprise Boards (CEBs) in the Republic of Ireland. Their role is to develop indigenous potential and stimulate economic activity at local level, primarily through the provision of financial and technical assistance, as well as ongoing non-financial enterprise supports. Each has a Board, usually of 14 people, representing a partnership between local business, voluntary groups, social partners, State agencies and local elected representatives.

Chapter 3

Media Content Analyzed

As described in the previous chapter, the content analysis provided an overview of the signifiers used in this particular sign system. A quantitative assessment of the medium and format of the place promotional messages was carried out and categories were devised to sort the different elements of these formats, which provided the smaller component units used for further analysis. This chapter describes the results of this quantitative assessment as a precursor to the more qualitative discussion to follow.

The media which occurred most frequently in the analysis were brochures or flyers, usually single page pamphlets, folded twice or three times. Just over 50 percent of the promotional materials were of this type (Table 3.1).

Table 3.1 Percentage frequency of occurrence of different media

Medium	% frequency of occurrence	Medium	% frequency of occurrence
Advertisement	0.4	Headed paper	4.3
Bag	0.4	Information pack	0.8
Beermat	0.4	Postcard	3.6
Booklet	3.6	Poster	0.8
Brochure/flyer	51.4	Publicity	1.2
Business card	9.5	Score card/ course guide	2
Catalogue	4	Swing tag/ label	8.3
Display stand	0.4	Web page	9.1

This is significant when Dilley's (1986) estimation of brochures is taken into consideration. In an analysis of international travel brochures, Dilley regarded these promotional materials as 'the closest thing to an official tourist image of each country: whatever image the tourist may have, whatever image some third-party company may wish to promote, this is how the countries themselves wish to be seen' (p. 64). In the current study, this premise can be applied to individual product promoters and the way in which they wished their product to be seen. As well as brochures, the argument can also be extended to include other promotional materials designed by the product promoters themselves.

The next most frequently occurring medium was business cards (10 percent), followed closely by web pages (9 percent) and swing tags or labels (8 percent). Only the home page of the website was downloaded for analysis, as the full site often ran to several pages and contained links to many other sites. In addition, only those producers who had their own individual website were included: many others had pages on sites constructed by others, e.g. their marketing group. The reason for this selectivity was that, in the former case, producers had complete control over the content and format of the web page, whereas, in the latter, producers often had to conform to particular conventions determined by others in their promotional design.

Other significant media included: headed notepaper; catalogues; booklets; and, postcards (all 4 percent). The remaining 6 percent comprised: customized score cards or course guides (used by golfers); publicity, i.e. 'editorial space ... written or presented by a journalist as a news or feature story' and not directly paid for (Morgan, 1996, p. 251); information packs (generally a folder containing other promotional materials which have been analyzed separately); posters; an advertisement, defined by the American Marketing Association as 'any paid form of non-personal presentation or promotion of ideas, goods or services by an identified sponsor' (quoted in Middleton, 1994, p. 154); a beer mat; a carrier bag; and, a display stand.

Significant proportions of producers were represented in more than one medium (Table 3.2). It was decided to include the range of media used by each producer in the analysis, rather than one example from each, in an effort to capture the totality of imagery and methods used in the promotional materials. Although each respondent used similar images and messages in each of their media, the extent and variety of content varied by medium. Business cards generally contained a minimum of information and were primarily used as reminders of the product and the owners and consumers were encouraged to take one away with them when leaving the premises. Brochures contained more detailed facts and descriptions and were generally sent to consumers and customers who requested information about the product. Catalogues were mostly provided to customers of crafts products to facilitate ordering and contained very specific product information. Swing tags/labels were used in a similar way to business cards, as a reminder of the producer of the product and also as a guide to product care and prices. Web pages often contained much the same information as brochures/flyers, the reasoning being that consumers with access to the Internet would not request brochures and vice versa.

The promotional materials were analyzed in terms of the format of their content and seven different types or units of content were identified: approval symbols, logos, maps, photographs, sketches, slogans, and text (Table 3.3). In general, the image being portrayed by producers was made up of a number of different elements. The units of content tended to complement each other, so for example, logos and textual descriptions of the property, regional attractions, friendly staff, welcoming owners or the craft product were accompanied with photographs, sketches and logos depicting these elements. Written text was the most frequently occurring unit of content overall, followed by photographs and logos. Approval symbols and slogans represented only 7 percent and 5 percent, respectively; minor proportions of the total, but approval symbols were present on significant proportions of the tourism respondents' materials. Many others simply listed approval bodies in their written text. None of the crafts producers' literature contained approval symbols.

Table 3.2 Frequency of use of different media (nos.), % of businesses represented in the sample, mean no. of media used by producers

	Region and sector (C=Crafts, T=Tourism)						
	Midlands		**Northwest**		**Southwest**		
Media (nos.)	**C**	**T**	**C**	**T**	**C**	**T**	**Total**
Advertisement	0	0	0	0	0	1	1
Bag	0	0	0	0	1	0	1
Beermat	0	0	0	0	0	1	1
Booklet	0	5	0	0	0	4	9
Brochure/flyer	5	36	19	28	15	27	130
Business card	1	7	3	5	1	7	24
Catalogue	5	0	2	0	3	0	10
Display stand	0	0	0	0	1	0	1
Headed paper	1	1	2	0	1	6	11
Information pack	0	1	0	0	0	1	2
Postcard	1	3	2	1	1	1	9
Poster	0	1	0	0	1	0	2
Publicity	0	1	0	0	0	2	3
Scorecard/course guide	0	2	0	0	0	3	5
Swing tag/label	7	0	3	1	10	0	21
Web page	2	6	0	6	3	6	23
Total number	22	63	31	41	37	59	253
% businesses represented	90	100	75	86	73	86	87
Mean no. of media per producer	2.4	2.1	2.1	1.7	2.3	2.4	2.1

Table 3.3 Overall frequency of occurrence of units of content in promotional materials analyzed (%)

Unit of content	% frequency of occurrence	Unit of content	% frequency of occurrence
Approval symbol	7	Sketch	9
Logo	16	Slogan	5
Map	12	Text	30
Photograph	21		

A more detailed analysis of the frequency of occurrence of each unit of content reveals interesting contrasts within the media analyzed, by region and sector (Table 3.4).

Table 3.4 Detailed analysis of percentage frequency of occurrence of each unit of content in the promotional materials analyzed, by region and sector

	Region and sector (C=Crafts, T=Tourism)					
	Midlands		Northwest		Southwest	
Unit of content	**C**	**T**	**C**	**T**	**C**	**T**
Approval symbol	0	44	0	41	0	19
Logo	77	24	65	44	84	59
Map	5	68	3	71	11	42
Photograph	55	84	74	76	59	59
Sketch	18	40	3	41	24	36
Slogan	32	38	3	17	14	20
Text	100	100	100	98	97	100

Approval symbols were used in the promotional literature of 44 percent of tourism respondents in the Midlands, 41 percent in the Northwest and only 19 percent in the Southwest. It emerged during interviewing that, for many tourism entrepreneurs, in the Southwest in particular, unofficial certification such as membership of certain quality marketing groups, citations in recognized guidebooks, word of mouth and reputation were seen as more important than official certification, so use of the approval symbol on promotional literature was seen as unnecessary.

Approval symbols made up only 7 percent of the units of content (Table 3.3), occurring 56 different times and the range of different symbols present on promotional materials was relatively small (12), with Bord Fáilte (the Irish Tourist Board[1]) symbols (the shamrock, 4-star and 3-star symbols) being by far the most prevalent (Table 3.5). This is not surprising given that approval by this body is recognized as the industry standard of minimum quality requirements. Most symbols were present on brochures and business cards, although a number were identified on booklets and web pages in the Midlands. The promotional materials from this region also contained the widest range of different symbols: seven, as compared to five in the Northwest and six in the Southwest. One reason for this was that, as a less well developed tourist destination, tourism businesses in the Midlands relied more on the certified quality of their product to attract visitors than the image of the region. During interviewing, many respondents identified signifiers of quality, other than approval by Bord Fáilte, as being of greater importance in terms of the quality image they wished to portray. Such signifiers, including positive media critiques, feedback from consumers and membership of certain private marketing groups, were often listed in the written text of the promotional materials.

Table 3.5 Approval symbols, by region, sector and medium

Region, Sector and *Medium*	**Description of approval symbol (frequency of occurrence)**
Midlands Crafts	None
Midlands Tourism	
Business card	Bord Fáilte shamrock symbol (4) RAC acclaimed (1)
Booklet	Bord Fáilte shamrock symbol (1) AA Symbol (1) Bridgestone Guide symbol (1)
Brochure	RDS Approved (1) Bord Fáilte shamrock symbol (12) Irish Farm Holidays Association (1) AA Symbol (1) IBRA Symbol (1)
Web page	Bord Fáilte shamrock symbol (2) AA Symbol (1) Bridgestone Guide symbol (1)
Northwest Crafts	None
Northwest Tourism	
Brochure	Bord Fáilte shamrock symbol (7) RDS Approved (5) Bord Fáilte 4 star symbol (2) RAC acclaimed (1)
Business card	Bridgestone Guide symbol (1) Bord Fáilte shamrock symbol (1)
Southwest Crafts	None
Southwest Tourism	
Brochure	Bord Fáilte 4 star symbol (1) RAC 4 star symbol (1) AA 4 star symbol (1) Michelin Guide 2 star symbol (1) Bord Fáilte shamrock symbol (2)
Business card	Bord Fáilte 3 star symbol (1) Bord Fáilte shamrock symbol (1) Bord Fáilte 4 star symbol (1) RAC 4 star symbol (1) AA 4 star symbol (1)

Logos occurred most frequently in the promotional materials of craftworkers, particularly in the Southwest, but were also prevalent among tourism respondents' literature in this region. Logos are used as a method of establishing a recognizable identity which helps 'to create an image of consistency, reliability and professionalism which is easily recognized by the public' (Morgan, 1996, p. 249). Businesses in the Southwest tended to be larger, more commercially or professionally orientated than those in the other two regions. As indicated, logos made up 16 percent of the units of content. This comprised 71 different logos, occurring 136 times in total. Of these, nine were abstract or stylistic symbols made up of random shapes or aspects of the business name or name initials. Another 12 were the logos of the membership organizations to which tourism providers belonged, e.g. the Ely O'Carroll logo (to be discussed in Chapter 4).

Table 3.6 Themes occurring in logos, by region and sector

Region and sector	Theme (frequency of occurrence)
Midlands Crafts	Connection to place/use of regional imagery (1) Landscape/natural environment(4)
Midlands Tourism	Connecting with the past (1) Connection to place/use of regional imagery (1) Landscape/natural environment (3) Membership logos (3) Product characteristics (6)
Northwest Crafts	Connecting with the past (1) Connection to place/use of regional imagery (3) Landscape/environment (3) Product characteristics (2)
Northwest Tourism	Connection to place/use of regional imagery (3) Landscape/natural environment (6) Membership logos (6) Product characteristics (3)
Southwest Crafts	Connection to place/use of regional imagery (3) Product characteristics (4)
Southwest Tourism	Connecting with the past (4) Connection to place/use of regional imagery (7) Landscape/natural environment (11) Membership logos (1) Product characteristics (3)

The remaining 60 logos were graphic images which have been described by Barke and Harrop (1994) as intended to 'implant images in the minds of consumers and ... aid in the recognition of some forms of corporate identity' (p. 99). These images or signs denote certain meanings to consumers and, at a deeper level, suggest multi-layered connotations. As discussed earlier, a logo or sign which resembles its object, e.g. photographs, is an iconic sign, whereas, in an indexical sign there is a direct link between the sign and its object (there's no smoke without a fire). With the third type of sign, the symbol, there is no resemblance or direct link between the sign and the object, the connection is purely arbitrary. Icons can also be symbols, however, when they are compounded with multiple secondary connotations, e.g. a pictorial representation of a dove is an icon of that bird, but also a symbol of peace. The 60 logos were categorized into a small number of recurring themes (Table 3.6). "Landscape/natural environment" and "connection to place/use of regional imagery" were the most frequently occurring themes overall.

Maps made up 12 percent of the units of content of the promotional materials (Table 3.3), comprising 16 different types of map occurring 145 times in 103 different media. As already mentioned, part of the rhetoric of place promotion is the perceived importance of proximity or centrality and maps are often used to convey this impression (Gold, 1994). Maps were used as directional devices and were present in only very small proportions of craftworkers' materials. Most crafts producers sold their products to retail outlets (to whom they delivered their products) or directly to consumers (including visiting tourists) locally. For most, therefore, there was little need to illustrate the location of their business for the purposes of directing people to them. Tourism businesses, on the other hand, relied on consumers coming from outside the region or country, so providing a map showing the location of the business in relation to major cities and entry points (airports; ferry ports) or a map of the local area was seen as an essential component of the information providing function of promotional literature. In relation to the types of maps used by tourism businesses, there were some interesting contrasts between the different regions (Table 3.7).

The number and range of different maps was much higher in the Midlands than in the other two regions, where the incidences were comparable. There were a number of reasons for this. Firstly, as emerged in interviewing, one of the positive images associated with the Midlands, as perceived by both organizations and producers, was its central location. One way of exploiting this locational advantage in tourism marketing was to use maps showing the proximity of the region to all major cities and airports in the country. The only crafts respondent in the Midlands to use a map did so for this reason in an effort to promote his retail outlet and workshop as a tourist attraction. In addition, many respondents felt that the Midlands had no image, so the use of maps (both of Ireland and the local area) was a way of combating this through illustrating the exact location of the region within the country and the business within the region.

As in the Midlands, maps of Ireland showing the location of the business in relation to major cities were also prevalent in the Northwest. Some respondents in this region identified a lack of knowledge of the area as a problem, so an effort was made to combat this, although less so than in the former region. Only half as many of these types of locational maps were used in the Southwest, for two possible reasons. First of all, this region was already so well known, both in Ireland and internationally, that many producers felt it unnecessary to indicate the location within the country and the use of local area, directional maps indicating recognizable towns and places may have been deemed adequate. Secondly, this region is the furthest away from Dublin, a fact that businesses might not wish to emphasize. Directional maps of the local area showing main roads and towns were most common in the Southwest. Again, this may relate to the perceived familiarity of the region and its towns to the greater public.

Table 3.7 Maps, by region and sector

Region and sector	Description of map (frequency of occurrence)
Midlands Crafts	Map of Ireland showing business location relative to major cities (1)
Midlands Tourism	Map of Ireland showing business location relative to major cities (22)
	Map of Ireland showing location of business (3)
	Map of Ireland showing location of the Shannon-Erne waterway relative to major cities (1)
	Map of Ireland showing location of the Shannon waterway relative to major cities and the location of the business on the Shannon (1)
	Map of the Shannon waterway showing tributaries, lakes and towns (5)
	Map of Midlands of Ireland showing County Offaly and business location (1)
	Map of location of the business in local area showing main roads and towns (24)
	Map of location of the business in local area showing main roads and lakes (2)
	Map of lake (1)
	Map of the immediate location of the business in the town (1)
Northwest Crafts	Map of location of the business in local area showing main roads and towns (1)
Northwest Tourism	Map of Ireland showing business location relative to major cities (12)
	Map of Ireland showing location of business (3)
	Map of Ireland showing location of the Shannon waterway (1)
	Map of the Shannon waterway showing tributaries, lakes and towns (1)
	Map of location of business in local area showing main roads, towns and lakes (8)
	Map of location of the business in local area showing main roads and towns (10)
	Map of river (3)
Southwest Crafts	Map of location of business in local area showing main roads and towns (4)
Southwest Tourism	Map of Ireland showing business location relative to major cities (6)
	Map of Ireland showing location of the business (5)
	Map of Southern Ireland showing main towns and airports (1)
	Map of location of the business in local area showing main roads and towns (19)
	Map of location of business in local area showing main towns (4)
	Map of the immediate location of the business in the town (4)

Even though many of the promotional materials contained some indication of distances to major cities or local towns within the written text, the vast majority of all maps in the three regions did not include a scale or any indication of actual distance. As maps used for promotion or propaganda can be used to distort space (Pickles, 1992), businesses could appear closer to various desirable locations, such as Killarney, the Ring of Kerry, Dingle, Blarney Castle and Bantry Bay, in the Southwest, as well as major cities and airports, generally. Also, many angling and cruise hire businesses used maps of lakes and rivers or included these features in their locational maps in an effort to attract the special interest visitor.

Photographs comprised the second largest proportion of units of content, at 21 percent (Table 3.3). Like a logo, a photograph is an iconic sign purporting to simply denote its subject. In fact, 'photographic images do not seem to be statements about the world so much as pieces of it, miniatures of reality that anyone can make and acquire' (Sontag, 1977, p. 4). Because they appear to have a more accurate relation to visible reality than do other mimetic objects, certain myths have arisen in relation to photographs: they supposedly provide evidence that something is, or that an event happened, as it is portrayed; they give people an illusory ownership of a past that is unreal; they allow people to take possession of spaces that are new to them and of which they are unsure; a photograph 'is both a pseudo-presence and a token of absence' (p. 16); they encourage people to dream, especially photographs of people, remote landscapes, far-off cities and the distant past; and, they create the beautiful and "picturesque" – because something was worth capturing in a photograph, it must be beautiful. Because of these myths, it could be said that a false photograph fabricates reality. However, despite their ostensible naturalness, photographs are as much an interpretation of the world as drawings or paintings, influenced by style, preferences and values (Sontag, 1977).

For Barthes (1977), although a photograph is not reality, it is its perfect analogue or, in other words, it is 'a message without a code' (p. 17). Photographs have a literal meaning as well as a symbolic one, because the relationship between the signifier and signified is an analogical representation and not arbitrary. This supports the myth of photographic naturalness, that is to say, because it is acquired mechanically and not by a human, a photograph appears to ensure objectivity. This denoted image 'naturalizes the symbolic message, it innocents the semantic artifice of connotation ... nature seems spontaneously to produce the scene represented' (Barthes, 1977, p. 45). However much they claim to represent reality, photographs are dense with latent meanings, particularly in advertising and promotion, because the signifieds of the message and the signification of the image are deliberate. Human interference in the photograph in terms of framing, distance, lighting and focus, that is the style of reproduction, are the signifiers whose signifieds depend on the culture of the reader. Codes of connotation are cultural, its signs are imbued with certain meanings as a result of the practice of a certain society, so the interpretation of the photograph depends on the reader's "knowledge".

A particularly good example drawn from the sample which illustrates the complex connotations which can be signified by photographs is that of the interior of an accommodation property (Figure 3.1). This image contains a multitude of different signs which employ a variety of iconic codes to signify many layers of different meanings. Some of these include: the composition of the picture, including the positioning of the furniture and the line of the wall-paper border, draws the view of the reader towards the fire place where a blazing fire signifies warmth, comfort and welcome; the tea-set and food on the coffee table also reflect this hospitality; the room is decorated in rich yellow, brown and red colours which echo the feeling of warmth and connote richness and luxury, a theme which is continued in the crystal decanter and glasses and gold candlestick on the table; the books (one open) imply learning and literature, while the piano suggests culture and genteel entertainments; the carved elephant ornaments on the piano signify exoticism or a well-travelled sophistication; the candlelight and vintage port intimate an opulence of the past; and, the flower arrangements symbolize refinement and beauty. Overall, the composition of this photograph was carefully arranged to connote lavishness, comfort and a cultivated elegance.

Figure 3.1 Photograph of the interior of a property

Eco (1982) provides a useful list of codes which can be used in the study of iconic signs such as photographs. For this simple analysis, an explanation of only three codes is necessary. Iconic codes often work at the level of *semes* only. A seme is the image or iconic sign (e.g. a girl, a house), which is in fact a complex iconic phrase (e.g. "this is the girl standing in profile"). The seme is made up of the signs (e.g. in a photograph of a face, the face is the seme and the signs are the mouth, nose, eyes and ears (Burgin, 1982)). Since iconic signs are recognized within their context, semes are the key factors in communication of these signs, juxtaposing them one against the other. *Iconographic codes* elevate the "signified" to the "signifier" of the iconic codes, in order to connote more complex and culturalized semes (not a girl or a house, but Little Red Riding Hood or a log cabin). They produce syntagmatic compositions which can be complex yet immediately familiar and classifiable such as motherhood, universal justice or the Three Wise Men. *Codes of taste and sensibility* establish the connotations provoked by semes of the prior codes. A flag waving in the wind could connote "patriotism" or "war", depending on the situation. It is convention which chooses one meaning over another.

Eight different themes were identified in the photographs present in the sample, four of which related to the crafts sector and six to tourism (Table 3.8).

Table 3.8 Themes occurring in photographs, by region and sector

Region and sector	Theme (frequency of occurrence)
Midlands Crafts	Craftsmanship and tradition (3) Functional information about the product (301) Landscape/natural environment (5) Praise/characteristics of the product (4)
Midlands Tourism	Connecting with the past (41) Connection to place/use of regional imagery (19) Functional information about the product (166) Landscape/natural environment (16) People (108) Rurality (1)
Northwest Crafts	Craftsmanship and tradition (10) Functional information about the product (71) Landscape/natural environment (1)
Northwest Tourism	Connection to place/use of regional imagery (22) Functional information about the product (80) Landscape/natural environment (21) People (55) Rurality (1)
Southwest Crafts	Craftsmanship and tradition (24) Functional information about the product (85) Landscape/natural environment (38) Praise/characteristics of the product (1)
Southwest Tourism	Connecting with the past (2) Connection to place/use of regional imagery (15) Functional information about the product (117) Landscape/natural environment (10) People (148)

Most photographs in the crafts sector tended to fall into the "functional information about the product" category (301 in the Midlands; 71 in the Northwest; 85 in the Southwest), particularly so in the Midlands, where photographs relating to other themes were limited (5, 3 and 4 in the other categories). In the Northwest, photographs relating to the "craftsmanship and tradition" theme were the only other notable category present (10), while in the Southwest, a significant number of photographs on the subject of "landscape/natural environment" (38) and "craftsmanship and tradition" (24) were also present. Although not specifically named, most of the "landscape/natural environment" photographs were identifiable, actual landscapes within the regions, particularly in the Southwest, and, as such, could also have been included in a "connection to place/use of regional imagery" category.

Of all kinds of images, the photograph is the only 'message without a code' (Barthes, 1977, p. 17) in being able to transmit the literal or manifest information without constructing it by means of arbitrary signs. This is different to the drawing or sketch which, even at the level of denotation, is a coded message, for three reasons: in order to reproduce a scene or object a series of rule-governed transpositions must take place and the codes of transposition are cultural (for instance, those concerning perspective); the drawing cannot reproduce everything so there is a separation of the significant (that which is included in the drawing) and the insignificant (that which is not included); and, like all sign systems, drawing requires a learning of the codes (Barthes, 1977).

Table 3.9 Themes occurring in sketches, by region and sector

Region and sector	Theme (frequency of occurrence)
Midlands Crafts	Product characteristics (2)
Midlands Tourism	Connecting with the past (2) Connection to place/use of regional imagery (5) Functional information about the product (79) Landscape/natural environment (6) People (6) Rurality (1)
Northwest Crafts	Functional information about the product (8)
Northwest Tourism	Connection to place/use of regional imagery (1) Functional information about the product (40) Landscape/natural environment (5) People (6) Product characteristics (1)
Southwest Crafts	Connection to place/use of regional imagery (6) Craftsmanship and tradition (1) Functional information about the product (25)
Southwest Tourism	Connecting with the past (1) Connection to place/use of regional imagery (1) Functional information about the product (74) People (4)

Sketches comprised only 9 percent of the units of content of the sample of promotional literature (Table 3.3) and these comprised a number of different types, including architectural drawings, artistic illustrations and symbolic diagrams. The vast majority of these occurred in the literature of tourism respondents, although promotional materials of craftworkers in the Southwest also contained a significant number (Table 3.9). Overall, 80 percent of the sketches fell into the "functional information about the product" category and most of these were of the product. In the case of cabin cruisers, architectural drawings were employed to illustrate the layout and specifications of the boats (Figure 3.2) and in relation to golf courses, diagrams were used to demonstrate the design of the various golf holes (Figure 3.3). Apart from these latter examples, artistic illustrations were primarily used in promotional literature as substitutes for photographs in order to reduce costs.

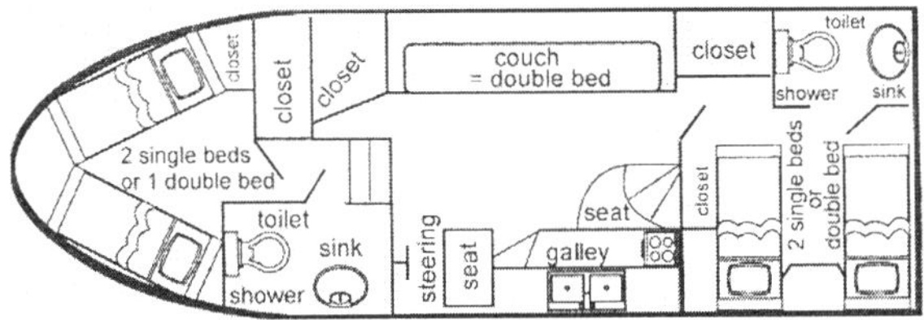

Figure 3.2 Architectural drawing of the layout of a boat

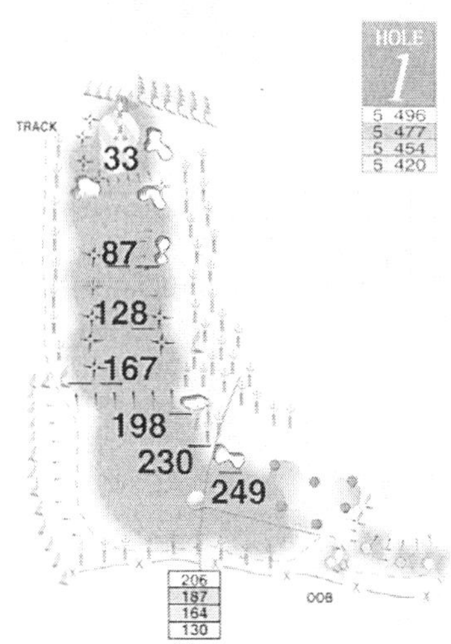

Figure 3.3 Diagram of the design of a golf hole

Slogans, defined as 'short, catchy phrases highlighted by font size, stylized print or position' (Hopkins, 1998, p. 69) were present in one-third of crafts producers' and almost 40 percent of tourism respondents' literature in the Midlands, but in lesser proportions in the other regions. Slogans are similar to logos in that they 'implant images in the minds of readers' (Barke and Harrop, 1994, p. 99) and are one of the most effective ways of doing so (Burgess, 1982). Perhaps one reason for the proliferation of slogans in the Midlands was that an image of this region had not yet become established in the minds of consumers, therefore, more producers used slogans to convey a variety of different images in the hope that some would become familiar. The fact that the largest proportion of the slogans used in the Midlands fell into the "connection to place/use of regional imagery" category supports this speculation (Table 3.10).

Table 3.10 Themes occurring in slogans, by region and sector

Region and sector	Theme (frequency of occurrence)
Midlands Crafts	Connecting with the past (3) Connection to place/use of regional imagery (2) Craftsmanship (1) Praise/characteristics of the product (2)
Midlands Tourism	Connecting with the past (4) Connection to place/use of regional imagery (9) Invitation to consumers (9) Product characteristics/praise (7)
Northwest Crafts	Connection to place/use of regional imagery (1) Product characteristics/praise (1)
Northwest Tourism	Connection to place/use of regional imagery (3) Product characteristics/praise (5)
Southwest Crafts	Connection to place/use of regional imagery (1) Landscape/natural environment (2) Product characteristics/praise (2)
Southwest Tourism	Connecting with the past (2) Connection to place/use of regional imagery (3) Product characteristics/praise (3)

Almost 100 percent of the different media analyzed contained written text, apart from one tourism example in the Northwest (a sticker containing the business logo only) and one crafts example in the Southwest (a flyer containing only photographic images). To a certain extent written text works in conjunction with photographic and sketched images to guide the reader's understanding of the images used or to direct them to the correct reading of the connoted message. In other words, when used with such images, '[w]hen it comes to the "symbolic message", the linguistic message no longer guides identification but interpretation, constituting a kind of vice which holds the connoted meanings [of the image] from proliferating' (Barthes, 1977, p. 39). This present analysis combined a qualitative hermeneutic approach with a traditional quantitative content analysis in the investigation of the textual elements of the media (Table 3.11).

Table 3.11 Themes occurring in written text, by region and sector

Region and sector	Theme (frequency of occurrence)
Midlands Crafts	Connection to place/use of regional imagery (40)
	Craftsmanship and tradition (38)
	Functional information about the product (68)
	Invitation to consumers (2)
	Product characteristics/praise (21)
Midlands Tourism	Connecting with the past (47)
	Connection to place/use of regional imagery (346)
	Functional information about the product (92)
	Invitation to consumers (20)
	Landscape/natural environment (18)
	Owner characteristics/personal service (43)
	Product characteristics/praise (65)
	Rurality (8)
	Tranquillity (19)
Northwest Crafts	Connection to place/use of regional imagery (20)
	Craftsmanship and tradition (36)
	Functional information about the product (112)
	Invitation to consumers (2)
	Product characteristics/praise (24)
Northwest Tourism	Connecting with the past (33)
	Connection to place/use of regional imagery (258)
	Functional information about the product (200)
	Invitation to consumers (11)
	Landscape/natural environment (26)
	Owner characteristics/personal service (29)
	Product characteristics/praise (49)
	Rurality (1)
	Tranquillity (6)
Southwest Crafts	Connection to place/use of regional imagery (44)
	Craftsmanship and tradition (48)
	Functional information about the product (145)
	Invitation to consumers (4)
	Product characteristics/praise (34)
Southwest Tourism	Connecting with the past (44)
	Connection to place/use of regional imagery (204)
	Functional information about the product (290)
	Invitation to consumers (7)
	Landscape/natural environment (21)
	Owner characteristics/personal service (34)
	Product characteristics/praise (66)
	Rurality (1)
	Tranquillity (8)

As indicated, written text was present in almost 100 percent of the promotional materials, running to thousands of sentences and tens of thousands of words. Therefore, a simple interpretative approach which implicitly employed the principles of hermeneutic analysis was devised in order to condense the units (sentences and words) of written text to manageable proportions. The written text of each piece of promotional material was taken as a whole and the various themes occurring within the text were taken as its parts, whether they were words, sentences or paragraphs. So, for example, in some cases, two or more themes occurred within one sentence, whereas in other instances, entire paragraphs related to only one theme. These themes or categories of meaning had been devised following an analysis of a sample of 60 pieces of promotional literature, as described in the previous chapter. Eleven categories were identified in total, nine of which were already present in relation to the other units of content. The two additional themes which occurred within the written text only were "owner characteristics/personal service" and "tranquillity".

In relation to the promotional materials of crafts respondents, text describing "functional information about the product" was the most prevalent by far in the three regions. This category included information such as the name of the business, descriptions and specifications of the product, contact information, titles and measurements of products, lists of the range of products available, business opening hours, prices, product care instructions, availability of gift vouchers, descriptions of packaging used, copyright declarations, terms of payment, order forms, raw materials used, year of production, lists of credit cards accepted, acknowledgements of support from various institutions and details of after-sales services.

The type of product produced by the craftworker influenced the way in which it was marketed. Those craftworkers who produced batches or lines of particular products (the majority of the sample) had to provide information, such as that listed, for the mass market. Respondents who produced custom-made products were more restricted in the information they could provide on promotional literature, details often being limited to encouraging the reader to contact the craftworker in person for further discussion. In fact, some of these respondents highlighted problems in identifying the correct level of information to provide on promotional materials. In order to attract the consumer, a certain amount of detail about the product was necessary. However, some respondents had found that, by providing too detailed information, such as photographs of the product or particulars of its specifications, consumers expected each individual product to conform to these. This was not possible in custom-made, individualized products which were often differentiated on the basis of their uniqueness.

Having identified suitable categories for analyzing the data and conducting a quantitative assessment of the constituent parts of the promotional materials, the next step was to analyze these components to highlight the ideologies and myths connoted by these media. As with all interpretative deconstructions of material culture, there are no definitive readings of these texts (Gottdiener, 1995). What follows is one interpretation grounded in semiotic analysis and it does not exclude other possible meanings. Logos and graphic representations employed by producers are reproduced for illustrative purposes but, for the sake of confidentiality, examples which could identify the respondent have not been used.

Note

1 In May 2003, Bord Fáilte amalgamated with CERT (the tourism training agency) to form Fáilte Ireland, the new National Tourism Development Authority. At the time of study, however, these agencies existed as separate entities so are referred to throughout the book as such.

Chapter 4

'Ways of Seeing' Countrysides, Landscapes and Rurality

All forms of communication operate within a cultural code where meanings are socially constructed. As discussed in the previous two chapters, language and pictures can produce 'ways of seeing' which are more than the literal meaning of the words and images and embody socially constructed connotated meanings (Berger, 1972). Place promotion draws from the imagery which already exists about a place, but it also draws more generally from common beliefs and myths (Hughes, 1992). Tourism, especially, has always been framed by particular ways of seeing. Numerous examples of secondary meanings which are produced by imagery arising from Western society's 'ways of seeing', in particular, rurality, countryside and landscape can be identified and several studies have explicitly explored these conceptions. Because my geographical focus in this study is rural regions, it is useful to consider widely-held notions of "rurality", "countryside" and "landscape" and examine how the promotional materials tap into and support these ideas.

Much debate has taken place concerning different definitions of the rural, ranging from descriptive, spatial and socio-cultural definitions and the social representations of rurality (Halfacree, 1993; 1995), to calls for the abandonment of "rural" as a universal concept and the adoption of a postmodern sociological approach to examine the ways in which places are made and the processes which give rise to "the rural" (Mormont, 1990; Murdoch and Pratt, 1993; Philo, 1993; Marsden, 1998). With the growth of rural tourism, the countryside has been 'commodified, promoted and symbolically consumed … But what the "rural" has come to mean in light of these changes is open to question' (Hopkins, 1998, p. 68). Hopkins (1998) observes that 'the "countryside" is an ideal deeply entrenched in the geographical imagination of Western societies… [it] is some other place, a place spatially, temporally and symbolically distanced from the everyday way of life' (p. 65).

The notion of a countryside ideal is not a new one (Williams, 1973). Bunce (1994, p. 1) uses words written two centuries ago by William Cowper, 'God made the country, man made the town' to highlight the idealized or romanticized view of rural life and landscape which continues today. This attraction of the countryside is a product of an increasingly urbanized society and has been constructed from a combination of historical developments and cultural values which have created a blend of ideologies, myths and images which have carried on the ideal. Bunce (1994) looks at the emergence of the pro-countryside attitude from ancient times through to the rise of urban-industrialization and examines the development of philosophical, social and aesthetic reactions to this urbanization. He sees it as an inevitable result of the urban-industrial revolution which produced extreme changes in society, economy and landscape and saw a massive movement of people from agricultural to industrial-based employment. These changes brought about a whole new way of life and created a large urban working class which is linked to the rise of a middle class of professionals who managed the new industrial system and sustained the influx of the new proletariat. It was within this moneyed class that the modern-day reaction to urbanization and the concurrent longing for the countryside first began. The rise of Romanticism saw changing attitudes to nature and rural life and had an effect on the countryside ideal. The form this ideal takes is based on a combination of abstract values and real images, symbolizing community and harmony with nature on the one hand, and on the other hand it is a collection of cultural and landscape images which stand out against urban and industrial imagery. Because the idealization of the countryside was created through historical cultural processes, the form this ideal takes varies from culture to culture. For example in Britain, it is argued that the countryside is valued as a landscape aesthetic (Nash, 1999), and this is reflected in its literary and artistic treatment and its use as an amenity. In the case of Ireland, the evolution and meaning of the image of the countryside is somewhat different, as will be discussed in Chapter 6.

Once the countryside ideal emerged, it was diffused through society by the culture in which it was born, through art, literature and, more recently, various forms of mass media. These reinforce the mythological and romantic images of the countryside and also instigate a desire to experience nature and country living in reality. We see this in various forms, from the country retreat to ex-urban residential development, and from the increasing popularity of rural tourism to what Bunce (1994) calls 'back-to-the-landers' such as New Age Travellers and those involved in arts and crafts for whom 'the farm is... a romantic locus for art' (p. 110). Also, elements of the countryside can be found in urban areas through shops specializing in "farm-fresh" food and "cottage" crafts and furniture. A positive side-effect of the sentimental nostalgia for the countryside is the growth in public consciousness about preservation and conservation of the very images which created the attraction. Of all the methods of diffusion of the countryside idyll, tourism is the greatest contributor to the maintenance of the rural myth. While visitors have long been attracted to rural areas and landscapes, it is only relatively recently that rural regions have become involved in developing, imaging and promoting themselves in an integrated way for the purposes of tourism (Butler and Hall, 1998). Mitchell (1998) identifies this as the second stage in the commodification of the countryside ideal. Firstly, the countryside came to be idealized, as described above, and, secondly, commodification of the myth has been boosted by commercial investment.

As Bunce (1994) pointed out, the countryside ideal instigates a desire to experience nature and country living in reality. 'Back-to-the-landers' were present in the sample of businesses interviewed for this study, where more than 50 percent were not originally from the area (Table 4.1) and a large proportion quoted a desire to live in the area and finance a lifestyle living there as the reason for setting up the business (Tables 4.2a and b). This was not just true for craftspeople; a large proportion of tourism settlers felt similarly.

Table 4.1 Percentage of entrepreneurs from the study area

Enterprise type	No. of cases	% from the study area
Midlands	**40**	**47.5**
Crafts	10	60.0
Tourism	30	43.3
Northwest	**48**	**48.0**
Crafts	20	30.0
Tourism	28	60.8
Southwest	**51**	**35.3**
Crafts	22	18.2
Tourism	29	48.3

In rural areas in general, in-migrants have been found to have a positive influence on non-farm business formation (Keeble *et al.*, 1992). In this instance, particularly in the crafts sector, there was a high proportion of in-migrant entrepreneurs, except in the Midlands. In general, crafts businesses can be quite mobile and entrepreneurs are often attracted to regions which have a readily available tourist market for their products (e.g. the Southwest) or have a reputation for crafts production or alternative lifestyles (e.g. the Northwest). The Midlands has neither. For crafts entrepreneurs in the Northwest and Southwest, business start-up was mainly due to a vocational choice to create craft work or because they possessed the particular skill or talent to do so (Table 4.2a).

Table 4.2a Reasons given by crafts entrepreneurs for setting up the business

		Region	
Reason	**Midlands**	**Northwest**	**Southwest**
Possess a skill	4	15	15
Vocation/Want	1	11	4
Became unemployed	3	6	5
Finance living in region	-	-	6
Demand/Niche/Gap	3	1	3
Other	3	1	3

As discussed, many of these were in-migrants who perceived these regions to be conducive to their chosen lifestyle: environmentally sound, rural, beautiful, the mythical West of Ireland. In the Midlands, where indigenous people were primarily involved in the sample, many started as a result of becoming unemployed or being unable to continue in their previous employment for other reasons, or because a niche was identified in the market. In these cases, it was not so much the craft itself as starting any type of small business that was the motivating factor. The reasons given by tourism entrepreneurs were more diverse (Table 4.2b), but a significant portion, particularly in the Southwest, cited a desire to finance their residing in this region as their primary motivation for business start-up.

Table 4.2b Reasons given by tourism entrepreneurs for setting up the business

		Region	
Reason	**Midlands**	**Northwest**	**Southwest**
Demand/Niche/Gap	8	10	11
Finance house upkeep	5	7	3
Finance living in region	3	1	5
To change lifestyle/business	2	2	2
Received advice to do so	3	2	1
Became unemployed	2	4	1
Other	10	2	6

The attraction of the countryside for an increasingly urbanized, industrialized society as identified by Bunce (1994) was utilized in the promotional materials of tourism respondents in the present study through references to getting away from it all ('an ideal location for a holiday away from town and city', 'separation from the outside world seems complete'), specific references to rurality, agrarianism and pre-industrialization ('accommodation in a rural tranquil setting', 'largely untouched by the industrial revolution'), and in relation to crafts, in equating handmade, artisan crafts production with the self-provisioning and working in harmony with your community and nature in rurality (I will discuss this theme in more depth in Chapter 5). References to 'getting away from it all' occurred under the theme "tranquillity". Although among the least prevalent of the categories of written text, its significance lies in its paradigmatic choice. In other words, within the paradigm of holiday experiences, the choice of this type of imagery unambiguously positions the product within a certain market category, one which does not cater for those seeking thrills, excitement and adventure, for instance. Examples include 'sit back, relax ...', 'in peaceful surroundings', 'You will relax and unwind as never before', 'absorb the tranquil silence broken only by the song of the thrush', 'an oasis of calm and tranquillity' and 'here one can find peace'. These images are aimed, primarily, at urban professionals and promise readers a relaxing, hassle-free holiday which 'will soothe away twentieth century stresses'.

As already stated, the form which the rural idyll takes, according to Bunce (1994) is based on a combination of values and images symbolizing community and harmony with nature and cultural and landscape imagery which contrasts with urban and industrial imagery. These are similar to the myths identified by Hopkins (1998). In his socio-semiotic analysis of the format, content and signs used to represent and commodify a landscape in South-western Ontario, Hopkins (1998) identifies the images that create the place myths of this symbolic countryside. The three most recurring myths include the naturalness of the environment, the connection to the past and the importance of community. These are the myths, the signs of rurality, which are marketed by the place promoters and consumed by tourists. '"Rural" is thus a marketed brand name for a specific kind of place commodity; the "rural" is a commodified sign of a symbolic countryside' (Hopkins, 1998, p. 77).

All of these countryside ideals were evident in the promotional materials examined. In relation to crafts, community was symbolized in terms of craftsmanship and artisanship, and the myth of handmade, rural production and providing for the community (Long, 1984 in Fisher, 1997). Fisher (1997) contends that 'associations of rurality and craft production converge, reinforce and compound each other … [and] pivots on the idea of "self provisioning and family enterprise"' (p. 232). The idea of community in tourism literature was exemplified in the numerous references to hospitality and friendliness in written text and in welcoming photographs of owners and smiling staff, as well as in allusions to traditional music, pubs and 'craic'. Within the analysis, most of these references occurred within the "owner characteristics/personal service" category. The different motifs which made up this category included declarations of hospitality and customer care ('the farmhouse with a thousand welcomes', 'the welcoming family atmosphere', '[Owners] insist on the utmost comfort for all their guests', 'let your senses succumb to the allure of our unrivalled hospitality and charm') and the use of the names or signatures of the proprietors. The former theme plays on the perceived notion of Irish friendliness, which has been identified as one of our most important selling points (Bord Fáilte, 1994). In fact, the 'farmhouse with a thousand welcomes' is an explicit reference to the Céad Míle Fáilte[1] greeting. The significance of the association of the owners with the product can be seen in relation to the use of photographs of proprietors, specifically, the perceived importance of owner involvement in maintaining quality standards and in ensuring a friendly, homely atmosphere and personal service.

The photographs used of the proprietors and employees of the business were usually very informal, showing smiling, welcoming faces. In the case of the proprietors, the vast majority of photographs showed two owners (usually identified as husband and wife in the accompanying text), who were generally casually dressed, in a relaxed pose (sitting or standing at ease), with the product (house; boat) in the background. The association of the product with the owners was an important theme in the promotion of many of the surveyed tourism businesses. In surveying, respondents were asked about the distinguishing features and quality characteristics of their products. Hospitality, 'homeliness' and personal service and attention, by the family as owners, were highlighted most often as the features which distinguished their product from others, while close supervision by the owner and personal input was the most frequently mentioned quality characteristic in producing a quality product overall. In the grading of specified quality criteria, the "close involvement of the owner" in the business was ranked most highly in general and particularly by tourism providers in the three regions. "Consumer perception" and "product/service differentiation" also received high scores. Given all of these factors, it was not surprising that producers wished to associate themselves with the product in their promotional materials, in order to connote these characteristics of quality, hospitality, personal service and 'homeliness'. The use of the husband and wife theme also signified the idea of family and domesticity, while the informality of the pose and dress connoted a friendly, relaxed atmosphere. However, despite this connoted informality, the general absence of children in these photographs reassured the reader of a professional approach to the business.

The employees included in photographs, while also smiling and welcoming, were rather more formal than the proprietors, in terms of dress and pose. Most featured were attired in clothing which denoted some type of uniform. This connoted professionalism and a uniformity or consistency of quality. Also, the vast majority of employees present were engaged in carrying out a task related to the operation of the business, such as collecting clean sheets, cleaning a wine glass or standing behind a reception desk. This, combined with the smiling faces, implied an enthusiastic willingness to perform any task to satisfy the consumer. Respondents did not combine photographs of the proprietor with those of employees in their promotional literature, as they suggested very different meanings. Whereas the qualities signified by the first type of photograph were those of informality, personal care, hospitality and homeliness, the connotations of the latter type were of a more professional (therefore less personal), albeit friendly and welcoming, service.

Another countryside ideal, harmony with nature, was very much evident in the promotional materials of both crafts and tourism producers. In crafts, it was used to naturalize the product and the production process through equating production with natural forces (Figure 4.1), through placing products within and on nature (photographs showing the product displayed on natural surfaces) and placing the product in the landscape (Figure 4.2). Most of these images occurred in photographs in the "landscape/natural environment" category. A number of recurring motifs were evident within this theme. Several photographs showed the product displayed on a natural stone or wood surface, sometimes with other natural materials such as fern fronds and shamrocks also present and framing the edges of the composition. There are several layers of meaning operating in such photographs. The association of the product with natural materials is an attempt to naturalize the product itself and disassociate it from modern, artificial, mechanized processes. The message is: this object is not machine-made, it is something of nature, using natural materials and it is authentic (the framing of the products "within nature" emphasizes this point). Another reading of the use of natural materials is to highlight nature and environment as inspiration in product design. The colours and shapes of the products mirror those of the natural materials shown.

The choice of the particular surfaces (stone; wood which appears old and preserved) is also significant. They connote an ancient landscape, enduring through time against elemental forces. The juxtaposition of such ancient materials with the craft being promoted, imbues the product with the same characteristics of longevity, antiquity and a timeless, natural beauty. The use of leafy, green vegetation again represents environmental consciousness and the signification of the shamrock evokes Irishness.

Another motif evident in this category was the use of one photograph, or a collage of photographs, of the product, superimposed against a landscape scene. Although not specifically named, these were either a generic landscape of a type generally associated with the Atlantic south-west coast of Ireland (Figure 4.2) or were of a recognizable, real place, which in this case was a view of the Blasket Islands from the Kerry coast (Figure 4.1). Such photographs attempt to signify similar meanings to those just discussed (naturalizing the product; ancient landscapes; environmentalism) as well as identifying the product with real places which are already embedded in the public awareness as desirable and beautiful locations.

Figure 4.1 Photograph of the Blasket Islands (product name removed)

In Figure 4.1, the movement of the tides and the setting of the sun also signify natural cycles and the passing of time, which is reflected in the textual description accompanying this photograph which refers to 'a [product] collection with a timeless beauty…'. The punctuation here also indicates that, like nature, the product will last eternally. The use of the word 'forged', which is usually associated with the blacksmith trade and crafts such as metalwork, equates the land with the product. It implies that, like the land, the craft was also 'forged by nature's artistry'. This metaphor further serves to naturalize the product and the production process.

Figure 4.2 Photograph of Atlantic coast of Ireland (business logo removed)

Figure 4.3 Landscape scene 1

Figure 4.4 Landscape scene 2

A third motif which occurred in this category was the use of a photograph of a landscape scene on its own (Figures 4.3 and 4.4). These photographs were generally accompanied by text describing the beauty of the scene and referring to the use of natural raw materials drawn from this locale or the service of this landscape as inspiration in product design. Again, the photograph as proof and as incitement to dream come into play here. On one level, such compositions suggest the message: this is where the product was produced, in this beautiful, natural environment, this is proof that the product must be outstanding. On another level, the reader is invited to imagine this far-off landscape, its topography, the terrain, the scenery and to associate the positive aspects with the product.

In tourism, references to unspoilt, natural environments and flora and fauna, and framing the product within nature in photographs (Figures 4.5) and similar sketches portrayed the harmony with nature of the rural idyll. For example, Figure 4.5 is a photograph of a Georgian-style farm/country house.

Figure 4.5 Photograph of old-style country house

There are a number of different elements of significance in this picture. First of all, the perspective employed allows the gravel driveway, the circular green area with the sundial, the hedge and the trees in leaf in the top, left-hand corner to be included in the composition. A full frontal view of the house would not emphasize these elements to such an extent. Also, a building on the right is omitted from the view, as it may have detracted from the projected image. The profusion of greenery in the composition and the vegetation growing on the walls of the house combine to connote nature and the countryside and to suggest that the product exists in harmony with its environment, indeed has been incorporated into nature (foliage on the walls). However, the neatly manicured lawns and the evenly trimmed hedge signify nature tamed or a gentle nature, which is in sharp contrast to the wildness of the environment portrayed in previous photographs (Figures 4.1 and 4.2). The message is that this environment (the house and its surroundings) is soothing, calm and restful, a haven of serenity within a stressful and hectic world. Also, in written text, the "landscape/natural environment" theme included references to rural landscapes, beautiful scenery and descriptions of the regions as unspoiled. Together, such images combine to emphasize ideologies of the rural idyll, country living and the landscape as aesthetic.

As well as this rural landscape imagery which stood out in contrast to urban imagery, cultural images were also evident in the form of allusions to traditional craftsmanship handed down from generation to generation, and nostalgic references to a past way of life. For example, many slogans fell into a "connecting with the past" theme. For craftworkers, such slogans conveyed a long tradition of craftwork and authenticity. For these respondents, their products represented '*Ireland... past and present*', were '*a thousand years a growing*' and there was '*History in the making*', in other words, a long tradition of craftsmanship had culminated in this product, which itself also became part of history. In written text, references such as 'the age-old tradition of the Celt', 'often handed down from father to son', 'a third generation Leitrim craftsman' and 'using techniques passed down through many generations' supported this idea.

Tourism respondents' slogans also invoked connections with a past time, in two ways. The first was to associate with a perceived myth of a bygone age of grandeur and noble elegance, where '*Formal magnificence,* [had survived] *from past to present*'. This was a time of stately homes and lavish lifestyles, it was '*Once upon a time... when dreams come true...*'. This slogan invokes images of fairytale castles and beautiful princesses, but readers can experience it now, because '*dreams <u>come</u> true*'. The other way in which products were connected to a past time was through reference to the old age of the property. Products had existed '*since 1209*' or were '*believed to the oldest* [product] *in the world*'. Such declarations of longevity connote permanence and a tangible link to that past time which tourists seek to recapture. In the Southwest, '*A journey through time*' promised this past recaptured, while '*Gracious elegance since 1897*', combined both connotations.

Cosgrove (1998) looks at the different meanings of landscape in a discussion of European cultural landscapes. A connection is identified between landscape ideology and the growth of European nationalism (Cosgrove, 1998). As the European nation-state evolved into what it is today, the territorial state become the principal geographical representation of spatial identity and loyalty. Therefore, the original meaning of "landscape" as a collective local community became impossible as the size of the "land" came to encompass larger geographical areas. A new ideology of nationhood was constructed, with language and landscape being its main components. Romantic nationalism in 19th century Europe used landscapes to represent the geographical unity of people. Irish nationalists, for example, used the pure, native landscape of the West of Ireland to represent the Irish nation before it became anglicized (Nash, 1993; Gibbons, 1996).

Over time "landscape" evolved from an idea of region and community to the more modern meaning of a view or scenery to which we relate aesthetically. Historical changes in the nature of travel contributed to this aestheticization of the landscape (Adler, 1989 in Urry, 1995). Before the eighteenth century, travel was based on discourse, on what was "heard" about places visited. This gradually changed to "eyewitness" observation, but still was primarily concerned with the documentation of information about places seen. By the eighteenth century, as travel became more common, travellers' observations, as distinct from those of explorers, were no longer recorded in a scientific manner nor expected to contribute to a scientific understanding of the world. Travellers became concerned with aesthetic rather than scientific evaluations of firstly, works of art and buildings, and then landscapes (Cosgrove, 1998). Bunce (1994) points out that because the idealization of the countryside was created through historical, cultural processes, the form this ideal takes varies from country to country; the different meanings of landscape in Britain and Ireland have been discussed. However, the overall notion of the rural idyll as a place spatially, temporally and symbolically apart (Hopkins, 1998) permeates Western society, the market at which the Irish crafts and tourism product is primarily aimed, specifically Ireland, Britain, the U.S.A. and Continental Europe. Therefore, it is not surprising that this spatial, temporal and symbolic distance was in evidence in the promotional materials examined.

Spatial distance was demonstrated through the use of maps showing, usually unspecified, distances from major cities and airports and from local towns and lakes. The spatial distance of the countryside from everyday life was also expressed through slogans and more general written text inviting consumers to visit these distant places. Slogans included '*A Day Away*', '*Explore Tullamore*', '*Golf in the heart of Ireland – sample the magic of the Midlands*' and '*Explore the Shannon on a cruiser*'. In essence, such mottoes conveyed an invitation (or, perhaps, a challenge, given the commanding tone of 'explore' and 'sample' rather than the more moderate "Why don't you explore" or "We would like you to sample", for example) to consumers to investigate the region and its attractions. The common usage of the words 'explore' and, also, 'discovery' in the Midlands in particular ('*A whole world of discovery on the farm*', '*Voyage of Discovery*') suggest the unfamiliarity of the region and readers are invited to visit this uncharted territory. Invitations to discover the attractions of the product in more general text were similar ('Come and discover the lovely …' 'Go and visit …', 'enjoy a visit to …', 'we invite you to stay with us in our home').

The temporal distance of the countryside from everyday life was illustrated in slogans, photographs and text, where connections to the past were made explicit. Evoking temporal distance relates back to Cosgrove's (1998) discussion of cultural landscapes. He points out that an important feature of the aesthetic attractions of landscape 'lies in their nostalgic evocation of pre-modern forms of collective life in productive nature. Imagined worlds of agrarian simplicity and social harmony are captured' (Cosgrove, 1998 p. 69).

The rural represents a 'liminal zone which is seen as occupying a ground between tradition and modernity and the societies they represent' (Gruffudd, 1994, pp. 61-2). Tourism promoters successfully utilize this attraction of landscape and rurality. Tourism is about escapism, escaping from the pressures of modern life, and rural tourism in particular is about nostalgia, re-discovering our heritage, both natural and cultural, and experiencing an earlier, more simple time, in other words, (re-)visiting that foreign country which is the past (Lowenthal, 1985).

A characteristic of (post)modernity is the 'museumisation' of the premodern (MacCannell, 1989 in Robertson, 1992). There is a growing tendency among post-modern consumers to romanticize pre-industrial times. Most see 'the world that was as a better place' (Lowenthal, 1985, p. 23). This is a result of the 'moral, social and identity crisis experienced over the past decades' (Laenen, 1989 in Goulding, 2000, p. 837). People idealize the past and contrast it to the stresses of the modern world and, whether recent or remote, the past is seen as 'natural, simple, comfortable – yet also vivid and exciting' (Lowenthal, 1985, p. 24). Lowenthal (1985) argues that the past seems brighter, not because it was better, but because people lived more vibrantly when they were young. A childhood remembered filters out the bad times, in other words, 'nostalgia is memory with the pain removed' (p. 8).

One of the reasons for such a nostalgic yearning for the past is a desire to escape from the present, favouring tourism to the countryside, for example. Crafts producers can also tap into this rural nostalgia as there is a long association between artisanal production activities and rural localities which relates to self provisioning and family enterprise (Long, 1984 in Fisher, 1997). 'This form of production is thoroughly woven into ... rural representations of the past' (Fisher, 1997, p. 232). In crafts producers promotional materials, connection to past traditions of craftmaking and craftsmanship handed down from generation to generation connoted authenticity and quality, something different from modern, industrial, artificial production as discussed above. In tourism, photographs lacked signs of modernity (Figure 4.5), slogans invited people to '*Step back in time*' and text offered 'the opportunity of going back in time'. For example, we can refer back to Figure 4.5, the photograph of the Georgian-style farm/country house. We can see that the abutting tower to the left of the view has a battlement which evokes a Middle Age tower house, signifying something ancient (although the size and positioning of the windows indicate a much more recent construction or modification). Another significant feature of the picture is that there are no signifiers of modernity to be seen, no car parked in the driveway, no television aerial on the roof, no electricity or telephone pylons or cables connecting to the house. The absence of such markers, combined with the old style of the house and the sundial, signify permanence, antiquity and a distant past recaptured. The two significations (a haven of calm, as discussed above, and a past recaptured) brought together reinforce aspects of the rural idyll, that tourism is about escapism and that rural tourism, in particular, is about a nostalgic re-discovering of a past heritage about experiencing an earlier, more simple time. The only vivid colour in the photograph is the yellow of the door, which helps to draw our attention to it. This is a bright, cheery colour which implies friendliness and hospitality, sentiments which are reinforced by the welcoming, open doorway. The reader is invited to step inside and experience the various connoted qualities for themselves. Apart from this example, the majority of photographs which fell into the "connecting with the past" theme related to one product, a heritage attraction in the Midlands. These included historical photographs of how the product used to be, pictures of the original owners and photographs depicting historical connections to the property. The purpose of the use of such imagery is to legitimate the existence of the product as an authentic heritage attraction (photographs as evidence) and to connote continuity and permanence.

In written text, the most common methods of "connecting with the past" in tourism literature involved: stating the age of the house or the period of history from which it dated ('A Georgian house', 'Built in 1740'), describing the history of the house, including its connections to the history of the area and the history of the family (owners) and invoking the past in various descriptive statements ('All the old world features ... offer a rare glimpse of a bygone age', 'relive the past', 'the spaciousness and elegance of an earlier age', 'Step over the threshold and take a step back in time'). The connotated myths symbolized in these references to the past are similar to those mentioned above in relation to slogans. This nostalgic revisiting of the past is one of the staples of rural tourism generally. It relates to the ideal of rurality being temporally apart, still existing in a past time, where past traditions survive and the 'filthy modern tide' has not yet encroached. The vast majority of the images examined simultaneously tap into, and contribute to the creation of, this myth.

As well as spatially and temporally, rural areas were also symbolically distanced from everyday life in a number of ways in the sample, most notably in evocations of tranquillity, peacefulness and havens of serenity. These areas were portrayed as offering refuges from the hectic pace of everyday life. Some of the ways in which this atmosphere was achieved have been discussed, including photographs of nature tamed (Figure 4.5) and written text explicitly extolling the peacefulness of these areas ('here one can find peace', 'an oasis of calm and tranquillity).

Another recurring motif within the sample of tourism literature which contributed to this symbolic distance was the depiction of "hidden houses" (Figures 4.6 and 4.7). For example, in Figure 4.6, the significance of the photograph of the property lies in the perspective chosen to illustrate it. The view of the product as seen from a distance and concealed amongst its surroundings signifies a number of different concepts. First of all, the placing of the property within nature, as discussed above, both in terms of the framing of the vista with foliage and the situation of the house among trees, is evident. Also, the view of the house is somewhat obscured implying that the property is hidden away from the world (again, a metaphor for a retreat from modern life) and the angle from which the house is observed implies that the reader has stumbled upon it almost by accident. The connotation is that the house is worth discovering.

A number of the respondents who employed this perspective in displaying their properties were members of the marketing group, Hidden Ireland, which was a clever use of intertextuality in their promotional message. The absence of a driveway and the closed door contrasts with the previous image, signifying that the house is less welcoming/accessible, perhaps more formal, than the property in Figure 4.5.

Figure 4.6 Photograph of a "hidden" property

Another example of a hidden property is illustrated in Figure 4.7. The artist's choice of what was significant about the scene, in other words, what to include in the drawing, expresses the desired meanings. The profusion of greenery almost obscuring the house and the absence of symbols of modernity signify similar connotations to those discussed in relation to Figure 4.6 (hidden from the world; seclusion; worth discovering; within nature; escapism to a past time). This property is also a member of the Hidden Ireland marketing group.

As mentioned in Chapter 3, artistic illustrations were often used as substitutes for photographs in order to reduce the costs of producing promotional literature. However, a well-drawn sketch such as the one shown, on fine quality paper (usually textured and in a pale or off-white colour) also connoted artistry and times past.

Figure 4.7 Sketch of a "hidden" property

The other symbolic distance evident in the promotional materials was the contrast between the natural environment of rural areas and the artificial one of everyday life. While not made explicit, implicit references to nature, unspoilt scenery abounding with flora and fauna, scenic country walks, and so on invited the reader to experience something different from their everyday lives, something more authentic (the real Ireland). In terms of crafts, the rural was symbolically distanced from everyday life through the naturalizing of handmade crafts production (as examined in relation to Figures 4.1 and 4.2).

The increasing popularity of rural tourism is an indication of the desire to experience country living and, as mentioned above, tourism is the greatest contributor to the maintenance of the rural myth (Bunce, 1994). As Butler and Hall (1998) point out, it is only in recent times that rural regions have become involved in developing, imaging and promoting themselves and this is evident in the growing involvement of local development agencies such as LEADER companies and County Enterprise Boards, as well as local, regional and national product marketing groups in promoting rural areas for tourism. Waitt (1997) alerts us to the fact that all national tourism promotion bodies have the authority to advocate landscapes that are part of the 'iconography of nationhood' both in terms of their promotion abroad and their part in the self-identity that connects people in an imagined community (p. 57). In his analysis of television advertisements of the

Australian Tourist Commission, he states, 'these advertisements are an integral part of generating abroad the imagined geographies of Australia and inventing the imagined community that holds Australian society together' (Waitt, 1997, p. 48).

Gold and Gold (1995) agree that 'tourism is one of the main ways in which a nation is represented to outsiders' (p. 202) and express concern that conventional tourism promotional policy, at least in Scotland, portrays only a partial picture of the country. This may limit a nation's ability to expand its tourist base, as well as develop other economic opportunities. However, it is not only at the national level that tourism promotion bodies can advocate particular landscapes. A range of national, regional and local organizations have become involved in place promotion to a greater or lesser extent in an attempt to publicize particular landscapes. In this context, then, it is useful to look at strategies employed by some of the organizations interviewed with regards to the commodification of their areas for the promotion of tourism and crafts.

The semi-state Regional Tourism Authorities interviewed all used very specific images in promoting the tourism product in their regions. In the Midlands, for example, the Midlands East Tourism label consisted of a representation of a castle turret and a round tower located on a green and yellow landscape, with a water lily floating close-by (Figure 4.8).

Figure 4.8 Midlands-East Tourism logo

This logo purported to symbolize some of the distinctive features of the East Coast and Midlands of Ireland: castles, mansions and fortifications dating from the arrival of the Normans in 1169 (the castle turret), early Christian monastic sites (the round tower), the green landscape, golden sandy beaches, and the numerous lakes in the region (the water lily). A regional brochure contained the slogans '*...where dreams come true*' and '*So much to discover and enjoy ...*', and illustrated regional features and products on a theme and county basis using photographs and descriptive text. The themes related to various archaeological and historic monuments, special interest and sporting activities and outdoor pursuits, accommodation and entertainment. Each county was assigned a descriptive by-line. In the study region, Laois was '*Naturally Beautiful*', Offaly was '*The Historic County*', and Westmeath was '*The Lakeland County*'. This organization also produced theme and product based brochures, such as *Holiday Breaks*, *Golfing Guide* and *Pike Fishing*, which contained product specific imagery (golf courses, lakes and rivers), similar regional photographic and text imagery (monastic settlement at Clonmacnoise, cruising on the Shannon, the Silver River in the Slieve Bloom mountains), and guideline maps. The production of the brochures and the promotion of particular themes in the regional brochure was part of the organization's approach to selling the Midlands in particular. As marketing resources were limited, the organization's strategy was to sell particular products rather than try to establish the Midlands as a branded place in itself, because, according to one respondent, 'people come to fish, or cruise, or golf, not to Westmeath'. Specific images were selected in-house by the organization and the countryside images especially were intended 'to capture the landscape atmosphere: unspoiled, uncrowded', but without being too barren, so people were shown also. The reason for this is that it is perceived that only certain types of countryside are attractive to the visitor, particularly those associated with the idea of "landscape".

'All landscapes are taken to be representations ... [which are] generally treated as something to be viewed' (Seymour, 2000, p. 194). According to Cosgrove (1984), the notion of landscape 'is a way of seeing which separates subject and object, giving lordship to the eye of a single observer ... [it] denies collective experience' (p. 262). This romantic gaze of the countryside is constructed by removing from the landscape elements which are not consistent with this particular view: people (residents, labourers, other tourists), signifiers of modernity (such as those discussed in relation to Figure 4.5 as well as farm machinery, mobile phone masts and so on), and indicators of environmental decay (derelict land, polluted water, rubbish dumps) (Urry, 1990). Milton (1993) distinguishes between what she refers to as "land" and "landscape". "Land" is a physical, functional resource which can be worked, whether for sowing, grazing or building and living upon. The utilization of this resource results in a closeness between people and the "land", which contrasts with the aesthetic conceptions of "landscape". A "landscape" is an intangible resource which is gazed upon from a detached and distanced perspective. As Williams (1973) put it, 'a working country is hardly ever a landscape. The very idea of landscape implies separation and observation' (p. 149).

The two Regional Tourism Authorities in the Northwest, Ireland West and Northwest Tourism, used '*Warm Wild and Wonderful West*' and '*To the waters and the wild*' respectively as their slogans. They both used photographs and textual images of their regions in an effort to convey an unspoiled environment and wide open spaces. Theme and product based brochures and booklets similar to those mentioned above, were also used by these two organizations. Like the Midlands East Authority, Northwest Tourism deliberately used photographs of isolated people in the landscape to differentiate the region from overcrowded destinations such as Kerry and Galway. The organization even had photographs altered to achieve the desired image, air-brushing excess people from the pictures. The stylized logo of this organization comprised a blue mountain, a green hill and a light blue sea or lake (Figure 4.9), representing the dominant natural environmental features of the region. Each organizations' regional brochure was also developed around counties and themes, somewhat similar to those used in the Midlands. In relation to the study region, the relevant by-lines were '*Leitrim - take a closer look*', '*Sligo - land of heart's desire*' and '*Roscommon Revealed*'.

Figure 4.9 Northwest Tourism logo

Ireland West Tourism's logo was very similar to that used by Northwest Tourism, consisting of a purple mountain, with a red sun setting in the background and a light blue sea in the foreground (Figure 4.10). The red sun setting in the sea has a specific association with County Galway as it reflects the line of the famous ballad 'to watch the sun go down on Galway Bay'. A series of regional product brochures was also produced, such as *Land of Golf* and *Walking in the West*, with the by-line '*The Heartland of Irish Culture*'.

Figure 4.10 Ireland West Tourism logo

As well as territories based on regional authority divisions associated with state funding, synthetic regions can also be created specifically for the purposes of developing a common image. Examples in the current sample included the Ely O'Carroll and Úna Bhán regions.

Ely O'Carroll Tourism is a regional product marketing group which took its name from the family who ruled this territory (South Offaly and North Tipperary) from the ninth to the 17th century. The name was chosen as a unique heritage feature which could be used as something a little different to sell the area. The image being conveyed was that of Ely O'Carroll Country as a distinct destination within the Midlands tourism product. The organization also believed that using a name with a history or story attached to it would afford greater access to publicity than would a more random name:

> There is a unique heritage here, we see it as a draw, something different. Ely O'Carroll is a key to get into places that we wouldn't normally [be able to enter], access to the media. The publicity you can get with a story is easier than if you didn't have the story.

In conjunction with the name, the organization used a logo comprised of images of a generic castle, a heron and water (Figure 4.11a). This logo was designed by a marketing consultant to represent history (the castle), the natural environment (the heron) and the River Shannon (water). The organizations' promotional materials contained the name 'Ely O'Carroll Country' in an archaic quill script (Figure 4.11b) and the by-line '*Get to the heart of it!*' on a background resembling an ancient parchment. A parchment map showed the location of the region within the centre of Ireland (Figure 4.11c).

Figure 4.11a Ely O'Carroll logo

Figure 4.11b Ely O'Carroll name

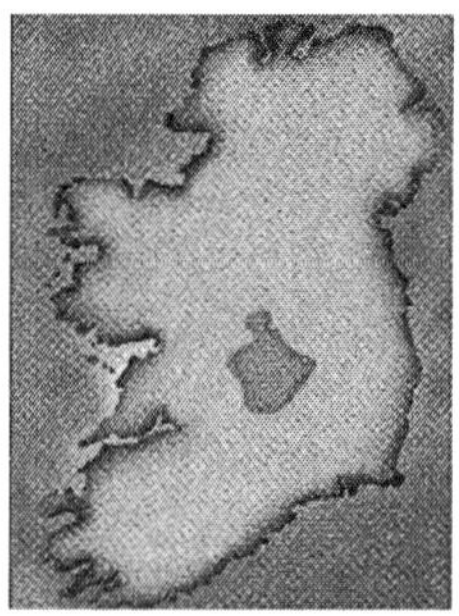

Figure 4.11c Parchment map of Ely O'Carroll region within Ireland

The brochures portrayed photographs of regional attractions (e.g. Clonmacnoise, an historic telescope at Birr Castle, cruising on the Shannon, Clonmacnoise Bog Railway, the Silver River in the Slieve Bloom) and people enjoying various activities associated with the area, such as river cruising, angling, golf, horse riding, cycling, walking and a traditional musician performing in a pub, as well as listing and providing information on accommodation, restaurants, activities, attractions and pubs providing traditional entertainment. The name of the group, the script used and the paper design combined to depict a region with '*a rich visible past ... in the heart of the Irish midlands*', where visitors were invited to '*experience the difference*'.

Úna Bhán Tourism in the Northwest used the image of a local romantic legend to link with local culture and create a unique identity. The logo showed the lady of the legend, Úna Bhán, looking towards Trinity Island on Lough Key (Figure 4.12) and the name was explained on the back of the group's guidebook as originating in

> the Bitter Sweet love story of Úna Bhán and Tomas Láidir, whose tale has been recited in song and verse, and handed on in Legend.
>
> *On Trinity the green leaves blow*
> *high where Úna Bhán and Tomas Láidir*
> *lovers tie.*
> *Each day the lark sings from the blue*
> *sky above bitter sweet song*
> *of their romantic love*

According to the legend, Uná Bhán, so named because of her long blonde hair, was the daughter of MacDermot, a chieftain of North Roscommon. She fell in love with a neighbour, Tomas Láidir Costello, but her father would not allow them marry and Láidir was banished from the area. MacDermot had Uná Bhán confined on Castle Island, Lough Key, where she went into a deep melancholy. Tomas Láidir, hearing of the situation went to see her, and when he left, vowed that if MacDermot did not send a message for him to return before he reached the river, he would never go back. The messenger was sent, but did not reach Láidir in time. Being a man of honour he was unable to break his vow and did not return and Uná Bhán died of a broken heart and was buried on Trinity Island. In his grief, Láidir used to swim to the island every night to keep vigil at her grave. Eventually he got pneumonia, and realizing that he was dying requested that MacDermot allow him to be buried beside Uná Bhán. His request was granted and thus the two lovers were belatedly united. Tradition says that two trees grew up over their graves and formed a Lovers Knot, which stood guard over the site.

The connection with the McDermot family was very important in generating business for the tourism group as the clan has held "gatherings" in the area; 'The gatherings of the family focus on the Boyle area and use the Úna Bhán legend in their advertising and include the Úna Bhán accommodation providers.' The connection 'has provided a network of international linkages for the co-operative and we receive queries to the website from throughout the world'. A dried leaf and flower collage purporting to represent the local countryside and designed by a local artist was the image used on the cover of the guidebook. Maps and textual descriptions of the region were also used.

Figure 4.12 Úna Bhán logo

Úna Bhán provided an example of an old image (folksong/legend) being utilized to draw together a region which heretofore was not an entity in itself, in a way similar to Ely O'Carroll. Both of these regions were artificially created as a means of marketing the tourist product within the region. At the time of the study, these organizations were at too early a stage of development to judge whether they would have any lasting impact on creating a cohesive imagined community within these areas, particularly as it emerged during interviewing that many producers did not feel represented by particular organizations' portrayals of their region. For example, many respondents in the Northwest study region claimed that Northwest Tourism should be renamed Donegal Tourism as this was the landscape it primarily promoted. Likewise in Roscommon, respondents believed that Ireland West only promoted the well developed and well known areas of the West, namely parts of Galway and Mayo. The low-lying lakeland landscape of Roscommon was not part of the iconography of the West, so did not fit in to its promotion. In the Midlands, most respondents felt that Midlands East Tourism did not in fact advocate the Midlands, promoting Meath and Wicklow primarily. These businesses were overwhelmingly critical of what they perceived as Bord Fáilte's, and the Regional Tourism Authorities', lack of promotion of this region. It was felt that the organizations concentrated their marketing efforts on the established tourism areas. The various private membership marketing groups, both within the region and nationally, were thought to be effective to a certain degree, but lacking in the financial resources and expertise to make a real impact. In general, tourism businesses felt that product marketing groups were more effective than state agencies in regional promotion. Another problem related to the paucity of promotion of the region in favour of Ireland as a whole and particular products. Producers wished to see greater, and more flexible, marketing support and training introduced, as well as better marketing of particular localities and products, notably but not exclusively, the Midlands.

At a more local level, problems were also identified. For example, in relation to Ely O'Carroll Tourism, many respondents did not identify with this image. Some felt that it better represented North Tipperary than South Offaly. Offaly LEADER also identified problems in bringing all tourism interests in the county under one umbrella. This was partly due to the separation of the county between different tourism authority regions,[2] which had led to the absence of a commonly agreed identity for the county. At the time of interview, Offaly LEADER was in the process of bringing all tourism interests together to develop a co-ordinated strategy for promoting the county and to reduce duplication. All of the state agencies and tourism groups were fragmented and developed their own brochures, websites and conducted promotion separately. It was a difficult process as each group had its own agenda and did not want to be taken over: 'We can't do a county wide branding yet. It's taken two years just to get the groups together, they're all terrified of being subsumed.' At a local level, Ray (1999) maintains that the "bottom-up" approach to rural development advocated by programmes such as LEADER, involves the construction of an identity for the territory involved. This endogenous development approach tries to connect people to place. It attempts 'to raise the consciousness of locality as the unit of development policy and action, and indeed as the geocultural unity upon which the meaning of development may be constructed' (Ray, 1999, p. 259). For extra-local "consumers of place identity" this place consciousness may also be significant in terms of infusing local products and services with 'the "personality" of the producers (their knowledge/skills, their territorial provenance)', so 'the knowledge of – and sometimes consumption of – other people's territories of belonging' becomes important (Ray, 1999, p. 262).

West Cork LEADER is an example of a local development authority which has attempted to draw its catchment area together into a cohesive unit through developing a programme for marketing locally produced food and tourism products and services. The fact that West Cork always had a certain distinct identity within the county assisted in this process. A branded identity, the *Fuchsia* logo, was used as a symbol of origin and quality based on strict quality criteria and codes of practice, and training programmes were provided to enable producers and providers to attain these quality standards. A private company was established, Fuchsia Brands Ltd., and West Cork LEADER funded a planned and co-ordinated promotion and marketing campaign to promote the *Fuchsia* brand which included brochure production, attendance at trade and consumer fairs, advertising, publicity, TV coverage, customer visits and market research (see Exhibit 7.1 by Gráinne Daly in Gibson and Nielsen, 2000, pp. 224-27 for a fuller description). The brand logo consisted of the purple flower of the fuchsia within a green circle with the slogans '*West Cork A place apart*' when used with tourism services and '*A taste of West Cork*' when used with food products (Figure 4.13).

The brand was used to promote the area as an indicator of origin and quality. Although not specific to West Cork, the fuchsia flower, in conjunction with the slogans, was felt to convey 'positive local characteristics such as environmental quality as well as the richness and diversity of the heritage, culture and landscape' (West Cork LEADER Co-operative Society Ltd., 1998). The fuchsia was chosen as the symbol for the brand 'for its bold and striking image, its ubiquity throughout West Cork, its positive association with the environment as well as its ready application in the branding of diverse products' (West Cork LEADER Co-operative Society Ltd., undated, unpaginated).

Figure 4.13 Fuchsia Brand logos

As well as the brand itself, photographic and textual imagery of West Cork (coastal landscapes, green fields, mountains, flowing rivers) was used in promotional materials, especially brochures, and the brand was also used on exhibition stands at various promotional events. West Cork LEADER in conjunction with the Fuchsia Brands Company promoted the use of the *Fuchsia* brand by providing brand usage manuals and leaflets, and by providing funding to those producers who had achieved the required quality criteria governing its use.

Other companies were also attempting to create distinct identities for their regions. For example, a LEADER company in the Midlands, Westmeath Community Development, in association with Westmeath Tourism Council, was endeavouring to give the county a branded identity through the development of a logo and themed brochures. The logo was based on the legend of the Children of Lir, *Oidheadh Clainne Lir* (Dillon, 1994). Lir was a member of the Tuatha Dé Danann, a race of people who appear in the fictitious history of Ireland, *Lebor Gabála Érenn* (the Book of the Conquest of Ireland), which dates from the eighth century (Ó Cuív, 1968). Lir's third wife Aoife was jealous of his love for the four children of his second wife. She changed the children into swans and cursed them to spend 900 years in that form. When the spell had run its course, the four children had aged and they died. Tradition has it that the swans spent three of their nine hundred years on Lake Derravaragh in Westmeath. The logo consisted of a line drawing of three swans on a blue lake with green hills and a blue sky in the background (Figure 4.14).

A number of walking, cycling and motoring trails had been established and themed brochures with maps, photographic regional images and details of attractions (varying depending on the trail) were being developed in conjunction with these. As well as describing the attractions of each of the stops en route, the brochures explained the Children of Lir legend and discussed mythological (the Hill of Uisneach, the ancient seat of the Kings of Meath since 1020 A.D.), historical (e.g. Fore Abbey), archaeological (e.g. crannogs in Derravaragh), and wildlife features of the county. Two product based brochures had also been developed, *Angling in Westmeath Ireland's Undiscovered Lakeland* and *Christy O'Connor Jnr.'s Guide to Golf in Westmeath and the Heart of Ireland* in association with the distinguished Irish golfer. These brochures all bore the Children of Lir logo.

Figure 4.14 Westmeath Tourism logo

In the Northwest, Leitrim County Enterprise Board used regional labels for both crafts and tourism. *Visual Leitrim* (Figure 4.15) was a business development and marketing scheme that brought together a number of quality vetted craftspeople and artists to jointly market their products using a regional label. The County Enterprise Board facilitated product development through grant assistance, advice and training, and marketing support incorporating brochure and catalogue development, attendance at trade and consumer fairs, directly targeting retail outlets, arranging a product exhibition in Dublin and establishing a Leitrim Design Shop. In addition, funding from a Peace and Reconciliation Fund was used to employ a person to market the *Visual Leitrim* arts and crafts initiative.

Figure 4.15 Visual Leitrim logo

Apart from its name, no other explicit use of regional imagery was made in relation to this brand. The logo consisted of the name with a symbol of a half circle in maroon and a green triangle, and the brochures and catalogues featured images of the products and producers. However, emphasis was placed on the fact that the products 'were of a quality and natural appeal you won't find elsewhere' and all from 'Leitrim's creative resources' in an attempt to establish an image of the county as a centre of excellence for arts and crafts, building on a presence of artists and craftspeople already in the area.

Leitrim County Enterprise Board had also been involved in developing a regional brand for tourism. The design was based on a bird figure, the *Heron* and the copyline '*Leitrim tempts you to take a closer look*' (Figure 4.16).

Figure 4.16 Leitrim '*tempts you to take a closer look*' logo

This brand identity was created to symbolize values associated with County Leitrim. The bird signified the environment, water, water habitats, and a sense of nature and natural pastimes. The word 'tempts' was designed to attract an inquisitive audience who had not visited the county before but felt they should (Leitrim County Enterprise Board, undated). The brand would be used on all the organizations' tourism promotional materials and the industry was being asked to support its adoption by using it in their own marketing efforts. Certain quality criteria were attached to the use of both labels.

In Sligo, a similar regional branding exercise had been undertaken. The brand which had been developed included stylized images of a flower, Celtic swirls and a shell (which was the direct translation of the Irish for Sligo, *Sligeach*) and the by-line, '*Sligo - land of heart's desire*' (Figure 4.17), also reflecting Northwest Tourism's promotion of the county. This was designed to be actively used by a marketing company, Marketing Sligo Forum, which had been established to promote the county. Its development was supported by Sligo County Enterprise Board and Sligo LEADER Partnership, who would also promote its use more generally. The brand reflected those traits which had been identified as being unique to Sligo - historical, cultural, natural, untouched, freedom (Marketing Sligo Forum, undated). It also reflected the Yeats connection to the county in the line 'land of heart's desire'.[3] Focus groups were held with consumers, producers and institutions to identify the traits to be incorporated into the brand, and consultants were used in its development (again, see Gibson and Nielsen, 2000, pp. 358-61 for a more detailed description). As in the case of Leitrim, only products which met certain quality criteria would be permitted to use the labels.

Figure 4.17 Sligo '*land of heart's desire*' logo

South Kerry Partnership also used a regional label in its promotional work for tourism. This organization had developed a series of standardized tourism brochures for communities in its area. These brochures were similar in design and layout using rural photographs and text to describe the areas. All brochures consisted of a common logo, '*Ring of Kerry*' in a Celtic script with a stylized picture of sea, sand, green mountains, sun and blue sky (Figure 4.18).

Figure 4.18 Ring of Kerry logo

Sea shells, sand, bog heather and a representative photograph of the area were also promoted on the front page of the brochure. The label and the images were designed to convey the beauty of the landscape and the brand was developed in-house with the help of a graphic designer. The regional label was also used by the organization as its own corporate logo.

The development of rural economies which, because of geographical and structural features, have failed to adapt successfully to this rapidly changing global environment, requires methods of gaining competitive advantage. Regional imagery has been identified by both the OECD and the EU as having important contributions to make to the niche marketing of the products of rural areas. The OECD (1995) has referred explicitly to specific landscapes, cultural traditions or historic monuments as creating territorial linkages which can function as a niche marketing strategy. The commercial value of regional imagery for rural economies that have become isolated from mainstream activity was also recognized by the EU Committee of the Regions in its Opinion document on *Promoting and protecting local products – a trump card for the regions* (Commission of the European Communities, 1996). Regional identification labels were viewed as enabling a link to be forged between the product and 'a region's landscape and culture' and it was stated that 'a region's image may contribute to that of products and services offered on wider markets' (p. 2). Regional images are therefore being defined increasingly as having a commercial value for the products and services of underdeveloped areas.

I have identified that support organizations can assist producers in developing such marketing strategies, although dissatisfaction was expressed by a number of producers with the images used by certain organizations. Tourism respondents in the Midlands and Northwest felt less than represented by their Regional Tourism Authorities and, at a local level, some respondents in the Ely O'Carroll area felt that this image was not representative of South Offaly. Organizations need to be aware of these issues in developing regional labels, to ensure that the images used are representative of the entire region, not just specific sections. Consultation with businesses prior to developing such imagery could lead to a more inclusive representation of the region in promotion and also give producers ownership of the process. This may also better persuade businesses to adopt the images recommended.

Notes

1 The direct translation of "Céad Míle Fáilte" is "One Hundred Thousand Welcomes".

2 The northern half of County Offaly falls within the Midlands East Tourism region, whilst South Offaly is part of the Shannon region.

3 *The Land of Heart's Desire* is the title of a play written by William Butler Yeats and first performed in 1894. The play is set in the Barony of Kilmacowen in County Sligo.

Chapter 5

Symbolic Meanings of Place and Constructing the 'Gaze'

An examination of the symbolic meanings of place in promotion demonstrates that myths develop which mark certain areas and objects as being "sight worthy" and that tourism, especially, but not exclusively, constructs people's views of particular places. Once a place becomes "sight worthy", it must be promoted as such, so places are increasingly commodified for this purpose. As part of the commodification process, existing images (real and mythical) of places are adapted and utilized. This can result in a very limited/stereotyped image of a place being promoted. Shields (1991) uses the term *social spatialisation* to describe this 'social construction of the spatial at the level of the social imaginary (collective mythologies, presuppositions)' (p. 31). He contends that space is not simply viewed as an obvious reality, but endowed with 'emotional content, mythical meanings, community symbolism, and historical significance' (p. 57). This in turn leads to spaces and places being labelled as particular types of places, which are deemed appropriate for certain types of activities, whilst other activities are excluded. It also has implications for the ways in which 'individuals and groups are located within, granted significance and or excluded from membership' of particular spaces (Nash, 2000, p. 27). Characterizations of places result from place images, which may or may not be accurate and which may result from stereotyping, oversimplification and prejudice. For example, in relation to the (mis)/representation of rurality, some commentators have pointed out incongruities between representations of the rural idyll and the realities of social and economic life in rural areas (Woodward, 1996; Cloke and Little, 1997). When taken together, a collection of place images produces a place myth, which in turn represents 'a more emotionally-powerful understanding of the geography of the world than that presented by rational, cartographic techniques and comparative statistics' (Shields, 1991, p. 62).

In relation to consumption, Sack (1988; 1992) examines the power of place in the modern consumer's world. He argues that consumption is a 'place-creating and place altering act' (Sack, 1992, p. 133). Products, like places, as well as having use value, are symbols which have meanings, and these meanings are primarily conveyed through advertising, the 'language of consumption' (Sack, 1988, p. 648). This language presents products as mechanisms with which consumers can create their own worlds and portrays a model picture of what these worlds could be like. Advertisers depict geographical contexts which frame these model worlds and these ideas become part of people's consciousness and beliefs about real products in real places, in other words, representations of places have practical impacts.

I found this to be the case in the present study in the way in which certain crafts and tourism products were promoted. In relation to crafts, images of generic, specific and mythical places were used in a variety of ways to depict a particular view of the world which consumers could become part of through consumption of these products. A particularly good example of a logo which embodies a number of different connotated myths is that used by a craftworker in the Southwest. The logo embodies the myths of an idealized Irish rural landscape, authentic traditional craftsmanship and the rural idyll. The logo consists of a sketch of a white-washed, thatched cottage with a wooden, traditional style half-door and stone path, set in a rural landscape with mountains in the background (Figure 5.1). The by-line '*Home-made in West Cork, Ireland*' was used in conjunction with the logo (as distinct from "homemade" which may have pejorative connotations, e.g. homemade clothes). At a denotative level, this sketch purports to be an icon of the workshop or home where the craft item was produced. Some of the product is sourced from outworkers who work from home and this is also invoked. However, the sign is loaded with secondary meanings which symbolize a variety of connotated myths. First of all (the order is unimportant as these signs are not linear), the connection to place is made explicit in the by-line, where the consumer is informed of the place of production. The thatched cottage also connotes a certain image of "Ireland" and "Irishness", one aimed particularly at an American market. This is the Ireland of *The Quiet Man* (1952) where white-washed, thatched cottages with red, wooden doors, donkeys and carts and red-haired colleens exist in an idealized landscape outside of time. This particular sign achieved its referential role metonymically (see Chapter 2), in that one sign (the thatched cottage) motivates the receiver to construct the rest of the chain of conceptions (*The Quiet Man* imagery) that comprise the myth (an idyllic, timeless, rural Ireland).

Figure 5.1 Traditional cottage logo

Another myth made explicit in the by-line is the notion of the product being 'home-made'. Again, the sign supports this image through connoting cottage industry, which in turn signifies authenticity, tradition and quality. This particular craft product is largely intended for a tourist and/or export (primarily American) market. The image of a craft product, home-made in a cottage in rural Ireland, works on two levels in these markets. On one level, it has been suggested that consumers' search for authenticity, not just in the product, but in the unusual (for them) conditions under which it was produced, is an effort to bring an element of distinctiveness or uniqueness to their own lives (Spooner, 1986). MacCannell's (1976) argument in relation to tourism echoes this contention: that tourists seek the authentic as a means of escaping from their everyday, meaningless lives and that "authentic" crafts may link the tourist/consumer with a place that evokes a more primitive life, untouched by modernity and rich in meaning. Littrell *et al.* (1993), in a study of U.S. holiday-makers, identified "cultural and historical integrity" and "craftsperson and materials" as major themes in the tourists' descriptions of authenticity. Authentic products were identified as those being genuinely from the area and hand-made in the traditional way using the original methods handed down for generations. On another level, for Irish-Americans in particular, the image is a nostalgic reminder of their roots, both real and imagined, harking back to the cottages where their grandparents lived simpler, more natural, self-provisioning lifestyles. This links into the third major myth connoted in this logo, that of the link between crafts and rurality.

Fisher (1997) contends that 'associations of rurality and craft production converge, reinforce and compound each other ... [and] pivots on the idea of "self provisioning and family enterprise"'(p. 232). The traditional thatched cottage of the logo is very much associated with rural Ireland at a connotative level, but this association is made manifest in the sketch which is quite obviously set in a rural, mountainous landscape. The significance of the rural/crafts production symbol lies in its paradigmatic choice which sets it up in binary opposition to modern, industrial/urban based production (see Chapter 2). The latent meaning is that the traditional craftworker works in harmony with nature and society producing only that which is needed, using non-invasive methods and natural materials as opposed to modern industry which is artificial, inauthentic and goes against nature. This in turn feeds into the myth of the rural idyll. As discussed in Chapter 4, an increasingly urbanized Western society has constructed a myth of rurality and the countryside based on a combination of abstract values and real images, symbolizing community, harmony with nature, wholesomeness, purity and a collection of cultural and landscape images which stand out against urban and industrial imagery (Bunce, 1994; Cosgrove, 1998; Hopkins, 1998). As Hughes (1998) points out in relation to tourism promotional materials, each of these 'genres of place representation ... produces as well as reflects the local geographies' (p. 30). The logo portrays a model picture of this mythical Irish landscape, depicting a geographical context which frames the connotated myths, at once tapping into these myths and reinforcing them as part of people's consciousness and beliefs about the place.

There were many other examples within the sample of crafts producers' literature which portrayed such model worlds. Sketches in brochures of cottages in rural landscapes connoted the ideals and myths referred to above. Photographs of generic and specific coastal landscapes depicted geographical contexts where the product came to symbolize the attributes of the place: natural, authentic, timeless and beautiful. This was especially evident in photographs occurring in the Southwest, as I discussed in the previous chapter in relation to Figures 4.1, 4.2, 3.3. and 4.4.

As well as sketches and photographs such as these, textual descriptions in the promotional materials imbued the skills of the craftsperson with the characteristics of natural forces and the craft with the characteristics of the land itself ('An epic landscape has been a million years in the making ... the craftsman too takes raw elements and shapes and hones and embellishes'), thus naturalizing the production process in contrast to the "artificial" methods of mass production. Landscapes and places were described, depicting the geographical context which inspired the design and production of the product, so the product came to symbolize real places. Much of this type of textual depiction occurred in the "connection to place/use of regional imagery" category and consisted of descriptions of particular place features and historical figures and events which had been used as inspiration or as the subject in product design, e.g. accounts of the Book of Kells,[1] Irish ecclesiastical metalwork, native Irish birds and the West of Ireland, 'dark, brooding clouds draped over solid but distant mountains', 'Inspired by the soft tones and greenness of Ireland', 'She lives ... in West Cork, where the natural beauty around her home inspires her designs'. Other textual images of place related to the use of local/Irish raw materials, '[t]he timber in this particular [product] is approximately 300 years old and came from an estate in [name of local town]', and to describing the location of production, 'the unique landscape and atmosphere of our boglands', 'We are located in the beautiful setting of [name of area]', 'Made in [name of town/ county/Ireland]'. The Irish language was also used, in some cases (in the Midlands) as a general sign of Irishness and, in other instances (in the Southwest), as a marker of location within the Gaeltacht[2] specifically.

The high incidence of images of place in the textual promotional materials of craftworkers in the Midlands is somewhat surprising, given a perceived lack of awareness of the region in the public consciousness among respondents. However, the vast majority were present within the promotional literature of only two respondents. Both of these craftworkers produced products with strong connections to the region; one used local raw materials and the other used regional and Irish images in product design. They also had the two highest numbers of media per respondent among craftworkers in this region. Although place images were not as prevalent in the textual materials of crafts producers in the Northwest, a wider range of respondents used such imagery, in particular in describing their location as inspiration, 'His work ... evokes all that is the West of Ireland', '... in the beautiful county town of Sligo where, like Yeats, he was inspired by the sea, mountains and lakes of the area'. As well as denoting the landscape of county Sligo, this last example also suggests a link to W. B. Yeats through place as inspiration. Predictably, in the Southwest, a higher proportion of craftworkers used place imagery in their literature than in the other two regions and specifying the location of production was the most frequently used method, '... crafted in the West Cork village of [name of village]', 'Your [business name] product has been made in our [town name] workshop'. Descriptions of the location as inspiration and use of the Irish language were also common. Reasons for this included a desire to tap into the perceived pool of positive images already established in consumers' minds about this region, as well as an attempt to market products to tourists by utilizing the rhetoric of place promotion.

Even more so in relation to tourism services, the 'languages of consumption' depict model worlds and places which are incorporated into the reader's perceptions and beliefs about real places. Again, examples have been shown of photographs which were composed in such a way as to depict a certain landscape which is of the past, welcoming and serene. For example, Figure 4.5 of a Georgian farmhouse imbued the product with these symbolic meanings through the composition of the photograph as discussed in the previous chapter. This motif of framing a landscape of nostalgia and tranquillity was a recurring one in tourism in photographs, slogans and text. Historical photographs and sketches showed how the product used to be and the people who inhabited that landscape of the past. Slogans invoked a mythical past of splendour and elegance ('*Formal magnificence, from past to present*', '*Gracious elegance since 1897*'), and referred to the longevity of the product ('*believed to be the oldest* [product] *in the world*'). Textual descriptions invited readers to rediscover that past time ('... offers the opportunity of going back in time to an era when leisure, grace and beauty symbolized the good life', 'All the old world features ... offer a rare glimpse of a bygone age') and to enjoy the relaxed, tranquil setting ('a place for peace and contemplation', 'an oasis of calm and tranquillity', 'absorb the tranquil silence broken only by the song of the thrush'). Slogans relating to the "connecting with the past" theme were more prevalent in the Midlands than in the other two regions. For craftworkers, such slogans conveyed a long tradition of craftwork and authenticity, meanings which related to the connotated myths discussed in relation to Figure 5.1.

A further world modelled by the imagery used by tourism respondents depicted a natural and beautiful environment, unspoiled and untouched by modern civilization. Textual references to 'the most beautiful scenery in Ireland', 'untouched nature, clean air and clean water', an 'undiscovered region of great natural beauty', the 'abundance of wild flowers and vegetation' and so on abounded in the promotional materials of respondents in the three regions, depicting remarkably similar worlds and tapping into Ireland's perceived image as a green and fertile land. The "landscape/natural environment" theme included references to generic landscapes ('the most beautiful scenery in Ireland', 'magnificent mountain scenery, lakes, waterfalls and miles of beautiful beaches'), references to specific landscapes ('the whole panorama of the Dingle Peninsula is revealed', 'the hills and lakes of North Westmeath'), descriptions of the regions as unspoiled ('untouched nature, clean air and clean water', 'an entirely unspoilt area of spectacular beauty') and references to flora and fauna ('an abundance of wild flowers and vegetation', 'the lakes, pastures, woods and bogs have a wealth of flora and fauna. Foxes and badgers, storks, ravens, hawks and kingfishers, orchids and willows'). These images combine to reinforce the themes of "nature" and "environment" and the connotated myths associated with them, as discussed in several of the previous sections, namely ideologies of the rural idyll, country living and the landscape as aesthetic. Logos, photographs and sketches used iconic symbols of animals, vegetation, trees, water, hills, butterflies and the sun to signify the green landscape and nature. An example of one such logo is that of a fishery in the Northwest which used an image of a salmon jumping out of water (Figure 5.2).

Figure 5.2 Salmon logo (business name removed)

This clearly denotes the product itself, but the fact that the salmon is jumping out of the water, and not passive, symbolizes a challenge (sport) as well as connoting health, vibrancy and a natural vitality. The image is also reminiscent of a fish caught on a line and thrashing about to break free. This suggests the myth of humanity's struggle against nature or "the one that got away". On the other hand, the fish is leaping from the water in the act of catching a fly (symbolizing fly fishing) in an ironic reflection of the natural food chain of which the salmon itself is a part. The angler is encouraged to participate in this natural process: the hunt for food. The environmentally sound connotation of the image is reflected in the copious use of green vegetation in the background; the colour green itself is significant in its association with both environmentalism and Irishness. The paradigmatic selection of the salmon as the species of fish is noteworthy. The salmon is perceived as the king of all fish and endowed with human qualities, symbolizing nobility, dignity and an almost arrogant eschewal of humanity's dominance. It is also one of the most commonly recognized fish, aimed at a wider audience than the specialist angler. In addition, in Ireland, the salmon has other connotations, those of wisdom and knowledge, in connection with the legend of Fionn mac Cumhaill. Fionn was the most famous of the leaders of the Fiana, literally "a band of warriors" who occur in the sagas of early Irish literature. The story of how he achieved his great wisdom by eating the Salmon of Knowledge from the river Boyne, as a boy, occurs in a text dating from the 12th century, *Mac-gnímartha Finn*, translated as the Boyhood Feats of Fionn (Dillon, 1994).

As mentioned above, representations of places, as well as being academically interesting, also have practical impacts. One such practical impact is when a place is labelled as a site/(sight) for tourism. In discussing MacCannell's (1976) theories on the tourist's quest for the authentic, Culler (1988) distinguishes between two types of authenticity. The first is that which lies off the beaten path and is unexpected, the second is that which derives its authenticity from its markers, in other words, 'tourists want to encounter and recognize the original which has been marked as a sight' (p. 161). These markers take the form of photographs, brochures, advertisements, guide books and so on, as well as on-site markers, such as information plaques. The markers identify the attraction as an attraction or, in Urry's (1990) terms, as a sight worthy of the tourist's gaze. Without a marker, a sight 'is incomplete as an attraction' (MacCannell, 1976, p. 112) or, in the words of the French writer, Prosper Merimée (1803-1870), 'Rien n'est plus ennuyeux qu'un paysage anonyme [Nothing is more boring than an unnamed landscape]' (Culler, 1988, p. 161).

This ties in with Urry's (1995) argument concerning the tourist gaze, discussed in Chapter 1. He states that 'the minimal characteristic of tourist activity is the fact that we look at, or gaze upon, particular objects'; the actual purchases are often incidental, so places themselves can be consumed, at least visually (p. 131). The tourist gaze is a result of people moving to, and staying in for a short period, new places which are different from their normal residences. This practice has become a mass activity and new services have been developed to cater for this mass tourist gaze (Urry, 1990). Non-tourist practices such as television, film, newspapers, and advertising construct the 'gaze' and provide the framework by which the holiday experience is judged. Tourists gaze upon features which are different from their everyday experience and these are captured in photographs, postcards, and so on. In fact, Urry (1995) argues that 'the gaze is constructed through signs and tourism involves the collection of such signs' (p. 133). Culler (1988) agrees that the 'tourist is interested in everything as a sign of itself, an instance of a typical cultural practice' (p. 155) and 'tourism ... [is] an exemplary case for the perception and description of sign relations' (p. 162). It is the study of these signs in the representations of places that forms the basis of this research.

There are numerous examples within the promotional materials examined of images which very deliberately set about constructing the reader's gaze of particular places or objects. In the case of tourism, in particular, certain logos and photographs presented a particular "view" of the place being promoted, framed in such a way for the reader to "gaze" upon. This encouraged the reader to come and "gaze" upon the actual place. An example of one such logo is that used by a golf club in the Southwest (Figure 5.3). A recurring motif among golf club logos was that of a coat of arms containing a number of different images relating to the product and the locale. The example given here uses the traditional heraldic sign format, with a central shield containing graphic images and a motto-bearing pennant below.

Figure 5.3 Crest logo 1

Various connotated myths are suggested in these types of logos. First of all, the very use of this format implies a long tradition/existence within the area and invokes the past, nobility and old, respected families. Golf was traditionally a wealthy man's game and the connotation of aristocracy associates with this image. The logo uses graphic and textual images with place connections. It is split into three different sections: a crest (the top section above the shield), a shield and a motto (Geoghegan, 1998-2000). A combination of different elements (colours, silhouettes, drawings, text) are used within the sign to evoke a number of different myths (heritage, culture, environment, scenery, Irishness). The crest and the chief (top section of the shield) employ a variety of icons (a seagull in silhouette, a drawing of a cliff and blue water) to associate with the sea and invoke the product (a coastal, links golf course), in particular, but also to provide an impression of a scenic view. The image purports to represent a real place or rather a real "view" which the consumer can come and see for him/herself. The reader's gaze is constructed through this sign and as 'tourism involves the collection of such signs' (Urry, 1995, p. 133), the reader is encouraged to come and gaze upon/consume the actual place. The colours red and yellow are used in the background and are traditionally metaphors for the sun, which symbolizes fine weather (Barke and Harrop, 1994). Green on the cliffs is reflected in the colour used on the base (lower section of the shield), which takes up most of the space in the logo. The connotations of the colour green have been discussed above, but, in this case, they also denote the golfing green. The white silhouettes of two golf clubs and a ball also signify the product being promoted. The positioning of the golf clubs in relation to each other harks back to the coat of arms format in reflecting a crossed swords symbol sometimes used on heraldic signs. The fess point (centre portion of the shield) contains three black silhouettes in the shape of the flower of the fuchsia, a plant which grows profusely along the west coast of Ireland. The seagull and the fuchsia combine to represent nature, especially a natural coastal landscape. The motto '*golf as gaeilge*' denotes the location of the product in a Gaeltacht area, but also connotes Irish culture and "Irishness" in general, which is also reflected in the positioning of yellow, white and green colours within a heraldic banner shape invoking the Irish flag.

A golf course, this time in the Northwest, provides another example of a deliberate construction of the reader's gaze. A coastal landscape photograph of the golf course from an aerial viewpoint gives a panoramic vision of the product and the seascape (Figure 5.4). A number of myths relating to photographs are at play here (Chapter 3). These myths include the photograph as evidence or proof that the place exists, the photograph as incitement to dream about distant places and the photograph as creator of the beautiful and "picturesque" (Sontag, 1977). These myths engender connotations similar to those discussed in relation to Figures 4.3 and 4.4. These include: the association of the positive aspects of the environment with the product, in other words, a product located in such a beautiful environment must be high quality (and must be a challenge as a links golf course); and, an invitation to the reader to imagine themselves there. There is also an element of constructing the reader's gaze involved; again the reader is encouraged to come and gaze upon or consume the real place. The implied message is "come see for yourself".

Figure 5.4 Photograph of a links course

Another way in which the reader's gaze is constructed was evident in a number of cases already discussed in the previous chapter, notably Figures 4.6 and 4.7. As well as providing examples of how the rural is symbolically distanced from everyday life, in these photographs, the view is constructed in such a way as to connote discovery, a happening upon the view. This was achieved through the use of the perspective employed and through the framing of the view with foliage.

The scene is partially obscured implying that the house is hidden away from the world.

Whilst Urry (1990) argues that non-tourist practices (films, television, newspapers, books and so on) construct the 'gaze' and provide the framework by which the holiday experience is judged, promotional materials such as those discussed do so even more so in a very deliberate way, presenting the view of the place and the product which the promoter wishes to be seen. Issues arise as to the extent to which such constructions create expectations and the degree to which these expectations are met by the product (Middleton, 1994). Also, as well as capturing the gaze in photographs and postcards, it could be argued that the gaze is also captured in promotional materials, particularly brochures, and that tourists collect these signs much in the same way as they would photographs, postcards and so on. So, prior to viewing the actual view, the gaze is consumed, then it is captured and collected in photograph, postcard or other promotional materials.

Within the tourist gaze, a number of different modes of visual consumption of the environment can be identified (Macnaghten and Urry, 1998), but two are of particular relevance to tourism (Urry, 1995). The first of these is the romantic gaze 'in which the emphasis is upon solitude, privacy and a personal, semi-spiritual relationship with the object of the gaze' (p. 137). The collective tourist gaze, however, 'necessitates the presence of large numbers of other people… Other people give atmosphere to a place' (p. 138). Examples of this include holiday resorts and major cities. Those engaged in the romantic gaze consider nature as "authentic" and it is by this mechanism that tourism is spreading causing tourists to constantly seek out new objects to gaze upon. Most professional opinion formers engage in the romantic gaze so this gets most publicity (Walter, 1982 as noted in Urry, 1995).

In the majority of materials surveyed here, it was a romantic gaze which was constructed and the products were aimed at consumers seeking this gaze. Emphasis was placed on showing views without people or with a small group or one or two solitary individuals in the view. One organizational respondent explained that this was a deliberate choice and that often excess people were air-brushed out of photographs in order to depict that desired solitary landscape; 'we have actually altered photographs to show isolated people in the landscape'. Also in written text, much reference was made to tranquillity, getting away from it all and peacefulness.

The photograph in Figure 5.5 is an example of the creation of a romantic gaze, as the significant feature of this photograph is the absence of people. This connotes seclusion, privacy and "getting away from it all", as well as implying that the product is awaiting the reader. This is a very closed image; the cruiser is among reeds, not in open water, appears almost stationary and the window blinds are closed.

Another significant aspect of the tourist gaze, according to Urry (1995, p. 139), is that it 'is increasingly signposted. There are markers which identify what things and places are worthy of our gaze'. MacCannell (1976) makes a similar point that a sight is 'incomplete as an attraction' (p. 112) without a marker. Very few objects are identified as worthy of being gazed upon so tourists congregate at a small number of places.

Figure 5.5 Photograph of a cabin cruiser on a river (business name removed)

Once a place is deemed worthy of the tourist's gaze, it must be promoted as such and so becomes a product to be marketed. Marketing is about 'identifying, anticipating and satisfying customer needs and desires – in that order' (Doswell and Gamble, 1979 quoted in Hughes, 1992, p. 39), in other words, producing what will sell. This relates to Sack's (1992) point that consumption is a 'place-creating and place altering act' (p. 133). Selling places for tourism thus involves producing a place, both physically and socially, in the image of what tourists need and desire. This has implications for authenticity, in that commercially motivated representations of place are not judged by their accuracy, but by 'the volume and value of subsequent tourist arrivals' (Hughes, 1992, p. 40).

This was particularly true in the present study, where the same actual or types of objects were referred to again and again. Within textual descriptions in the "connection to place/use of regional imagery category", the most frequently occurring theme in the three regions was listing or describing local or regional attractions and facilities. In the Midlands, for example, one would be excused for believing that the only features present in the region were the Shannon River, the Slieve Bloom mountains, Clonmacnoise and, to a lesser extent, Birr Castle, whilst golf, horse riding and fishing were the recreational activities referred to most often. In the Northwest, the River Shannon, or the Shannon-Erne Waterway, was the most frequently mentioned regional attraction, whilst golf, fishing and horse riding were again the most commonly quoted activities. References to a variety of archaeological and historical sites were also recurrent in both regions. It would appear, in textual descriptions at least, that similar images were being portrayed of both of these regions. In the Southwest, the most frequently mentioned attractions were the Ring of Kerry and the Dingle Peninsula. Watersports, fishing and horse riding were the most commonly referenced activities.

In this "connection to place/use of regional imagery" category, there were two main types of photograph present, comprising images of regional landscapes and of cultural features (incorporating archaeological, architectural, artistic and historical elements). In the Northwest and Southwest, landscape images outnumbered cultural images threefold, while in the Midlands, the latter were slightly more numerous than the former. The large proportion of landscape images in the Northwest was inflated by the presence of one booklet promoting a specific area which included over 80 percent of this sample. In the Southwest, the perceived awareness of this region in the public consciousness undoubtedly contributed to the greater use of landscape imagery in the region, whilst in the Midlands, the converse was true.

The specific regional images which occurred most frequently in the Midlands sample were photographs of the early Christian monastic site at Clonmacnoise and the River Shannon (Figures 5.6 and 5.7).

Figure 5.6 Clonmacnoise

Figure 5.7 The Shannon River at Athlone

In the Northwest, no one regional image was included more regularly than others, apart from Lough Gill (Figure 5.8) which occurred twice in the booklet mentioned above. Bantry Bay (Figure 5.9) and Mizen Head, in particular the suspension bridge at the latter (Figure 5.10), were the most frequently occurring regional features in the Southwest, but they were primarily used by two respondents.

Figure 5.8 Photograph of Lough Gill

Figure 5.9 Photograph of Bantry Bay

Figure 5.10 Photograph of Mizen Head

When all of the different types or units of content are taken together (approval symbols, logos, maps, photographs, sketches, slogans, and text), it is evident that in all three regions, much emphasis was placed on archaeological and heritage attractions and landscape, notably rural, coastal, lakeland or mountainous landscapes. Little or no reference was made to urban landscapes, towns, farmland, industrial sites or sporting events, which all exist within the regions, but have been deemed unworthy of the tourist's gaze.

Whilst Urry's arguments related to tourism primarily, certain elements could also be applied to crafts products, particularly in relation to constructing the gaze. In the crafts sector, most of the photographs fell into the "functional information about the product" category and the vast majority of these were of the product standing alone, particularly in catalogues and brochures/flyers. The purpose of these photographs was to show the product to the consumer in the best way possible and many such photographs represent very deliberate attempts to construct the reader's gaze. Products were shown against a particular colour background redolent of portrait photography, and framed in such a way as to encourage the consumer to gaze upon the craft almost as an *object d'art* (Figure 5.11). In order to do this, most were framed with a black or grey border, which helped to make the photograph more prominent on the page, and were set against a background of a one-colour, horizontal light-to-dark gradient, reminiscent of the back-drop used by professional portrait photographers. The colour used in the background complemented the colour of the product or was drawn from the same part of the colour spectrum, so a grey, blue or black product would have a background similar to that shown below.

Figure 5.11 Background used in photographs of "stand alone" crafts products

The colour was gradated so as to add to the definition of the product. These elements (the frame and back-drop) combined to represent the product as being aesthetically pleasing, a work of art and professionally presented.

Another way in which the reader's gaze was constructed in relation to crafts items was to portray the product in its final setting, e.g. a sculpture in a place of prominence outside a public building, a chair in a room by a window, a framed picture hanging on a patterned wall, next to a curtain. As discussed above, part of the mythology of photographs is to encourage the reader to fantasize about places or things outside of their own experience, things they have not seen before. The purpose of placing the product in its ultimate (natural) setting is to assist the reader's imagination in this process. It also highlights the functional characteristics of the product and implies that it is being used (the myth of the photograph as proof of an event).

The consumption of crafts products also fits in with Urry's (1995) theory on the 'end of tourism' (p. 148). He believes that people are engaged in what might be called tourism practices much of the time, whether they are actually travelling or not through the multiplicity of signs which constantly surround them and the 'aestheticization of everyday life' (p. 149). Promotion and consumption of crafts products is part of this process, especially those which use place imagery/ connection to place as a marketing strategy. Whether it is through utilizing local raw materials, the use of place imagery in product design, through naming a product after a place or through the use of the landscape as inspiration in artistic endeavour (examples of all of which are present in the sample), consumers of these products are encouraged to buy/consume part of that place through the purchase of the craft product, much as they would be if the product were being purchased in the place as a souvenir. With the use of place imagery in product promotion, consumers of crafts can purchase souvenirs without every having actually visited the place.

Fleming and Roth (1991) have identified three types of place images that feature in advertising: actual places, generic places and fictional places. Actual or specific places are drawn from depictions or representations of real landscapes. The particulars are important in that these are readily identifiable places; Fleming and Roth (1991) give the example of the Cathedral of Notre Dame in Paris, but in another sense they may be just representative of what is to be seen in a particular area. Generic places symbolize a type of place, e.g. mountains, lakes, city streets, farms, beaches and forests, and are often used by advertisers to reach a wide audience. Fleming and Roth (1991) observe that certain generic landscapes symbolize certain countries or regions, e.g. the green fields of Ireland. Fictitious places are imaginary places of the future, of legends, of dreams, or are deliberately unidentifiable. Some advertisements may use actual place images with a slogan that describes an imaginary place, e.g. 'Hawaii – paradise for all seasons... Denmark – we invented once upon a time' (p. 288). Fleming and Roth (1991) conclude by noting that place images can be very symbolic, that some places are very widely recognized and that 'place itself can be used as a metaphor for a lifestyle or an emotion' (p. 291).

Examples of the use of each of these actual, generic and fictional types of place have been identified within the sample of both crafts and tourism promotional literature. Actual place images were used more frequently in tourism promotion than in crafts. Such images were used generally to portray the attractions in a region, e.g. photographs of Clonmacnoise and Knocknarea, textual references to Bantry Bay, the lakes of Killarney, the Slieve Bloom mountains, and so on. In crafts, very few actual place images were used. Exceptions were evident in the Southwest, where photographs of recognizably Southwestern images, such as the Blasket Islands (Figure 4.1), were used and references were made in text to the local place of production ('We are located in the beautiful setting of [name of area]', 'crafted in the West Cork village of [name of village]'). This was partly to take advantage of these well-known places and partly to appeal to tourists as consumers.

Generic place images were used by both sectors. In crafts such images were used to place the product in a rural, bog or coastal landscape in order to imbue the product with the characteristics of the land, to naturalize its production and to promote its authenticity (again, see Chapter 4 in relation to Figures 4.3 and 4.4). In tourism promotion, generic images were shown to portray beautiful scenery, natural unspoilt environments in photographs and written text; 'the most beautiful scenery in Ireland', ' "Oh, the quiet, the green of the grass, the grey willows, The light, and the shine, and the air sweet and free!' Walter de la Mare – 'I Dream of a Place" ', 'A land of clean air and dramatic skies'.

References to fictional places were evident in logos, slogans and written text. In crafts, for example, the logo of the thatched cottage (Figure 5.1) connoted an idealized Irish rural landscape out of time, the fictional land of *The Quiet Man*. In tourism, nostalgic references to the past connoted places which existed in a fictional past time where life was simpler, more natural and more innocent. The connotations of photographs such as Figure 4.5 of the Georgian farmhouse and slogans depicting a past of '*Gracious elegance…*' have been discussed above. Written text, in particular, created a fictional world of olden times; readers were invited to 'come and experience the beauty and elegance of a bygone age', products 'possesse[d] the charm of an earlier era', and readers could 'journey through time' and 'step back in time. Banish the cares of today, surrender to the gracious living of a forgotten age'.

Fleming and Roth (1991) also note that places can be symbolic, which again was shown to be true in the sampled literature. In crafts, for example, the photographs of the Atlantic seascape (Figure 4.2) and the Blasket Islands, '*a land forged by nature's artistry*' (Figure 4.1), and more explicit textual connections between the craftworker and nature ('An epic landscape has been a million years in the making… the craftsman too takes raw elements and shapes and hones and embellishes'), symbolized and naturalized the artistry of the craftworker as he forged his craft. In relation to tourism products, I identified two businesses in the Northwest which utilized symbolic place images of County Sligo as metaphors for their products. Photographs of Knocknarea and references to, and photographs of, archaeological and historical sites symbolized an historic accommodation property and a magical and mythical land steeped in legend and literature.

These tourism businesses were both accommodation enterprises and can be acknowledged as examples of best practice in the use of place imagery in their promotion. Business A was a heritage house dating from the 17th century, newly renovated and restored by the present owner, the tenth generation of the family to inhabit the property. The product had strong connections to the region and the history of the product and the owners was interwoven with the history of the area, so the property itself was an image of the region. Business B, on the other hand, was a purpose built hotel which used the local place name as the business name and various images of the region in product promotion.

The present owner of Business A had previously operated a restaurant in a local town and, with its success, decided to expand the business. He bought the property, which had been empty for many years, from his brother and restored the interior which had suffered neglect. He established the business initially as a restaurant, but eventually added bedrooms and a bar. Heritage Council support was received for restoration work and European Regional Development Fund funding was obtained for extending the accommodation premises. At the time of interview, the product consisted of a 30 bedroom hotel, employing 14 full-time, 10 part-time and six seasonal staff, excluding the owner.

When the business was first established, the market was a local one so promotion consisted of advertising in local media. As the accommodation was added, additional promotional methods were introduced, including brochure distribution to local businesses, attendance at trade fairs and Bord Fáilte led trade workshops, membership of a variety of marketing organizations, advertising in various guide books and the development of a website, through which visitors could make bookings. However, the respondent believed, like many others, that personal recommendation was the most productive method overall.

The owner perceived that it was the architecture and the history of the house which distinguished it from other accommodation properties and images of the historical and archaeological heritage of the region were used in promotion, because they were felt to 'fit in with the image we're trying to project'. A photograph of megalithic remains at Carrowmore (the largest cemetery of megalithic tombs in Ireland) with Ben Bulben in the background (Figure 5.12) was used in conjunction with textual references to Lisadell House, Yeats' Grave at Drumcliff, the "Yeats Country" and Knocknarea and Ben Bulben mountains.

Also, in describing the history of the property, reference was made to famous visitors to the house, including Lady Gregory and W. B. Yeats. Other "connection to place" motifs included a description of the house as 'the perfect base for your visit to the West of Ireland', as lying 'in the romantic landscape where the poet Yeats found his inspiration, north of awe-inspiring Connemara and south of the beautiful Donegal coast' and references to beaches, golf, fishing, Lough Gill, Lough Arrow and 'a marvellous varied countryside for touring and walking'.

Other themes evident included descriptions of the immediate location of the house in 'lovely gardens stretching down to the Unsin river and hundreds of acres of woods and meadows to walk in', evocations of tranquillity ('For the holiday maker there is peace and quiet'), connections with the past ('The tale of [product name] is a wonderful journey through time'), and references such as 'romantic landscape', Knocknarea, 'journey through time' and Yeats Country connoted a mystical, mythical place. The promotional literature of Business A provides a useful example of how a number of different themes combine to convey an overall image of a relaxing and fascinating holiday experience in a house steeped in history in a fantastic land.

This "mythical land" theme is also evident in Business B's promotional material. This small hotel had a limited marketing budget as compared to larger hotels and only one piece of literature was included in the sample. However, this full-colour brochure afforded a particularly good example of the use of place imagery to promote an accommodation product. The hotel was a family owned business, established 29 years prior to the interview by the parents of the current owners. Over time the accommodation increased from 10 to 25 bedrooms and the business grew to employ 15 full-time and 10 seasonal staff. No external assistance was received, financial or otherwise, from any support body.

Figure 5.12 Carrowmore with Ben Bulben in background

From the beginning, as a small hotel, the unique selling point was the personal attention given to every guest. Initial marketing involved attendance at trade fairs in Dublin and Belfast and advertising in national newspapers. The owners then became founder members of a national marketing group which became involved in international marketing. The business also produced a brochure, targeted tour operators and the corporate market through direct mail shots and were listed in Bord Fáilte and Irish Hotel Federation guide books. The hotel was named after the local townland 'because that was the done thing at the time'. However, a more conscious use of photographic and textual imagery is evident in the hotel's current brochure.

The front page consists of a photograph of the building, as seen from a distance, with the view partly framed by foliage and with well-manicured lawns and trees in the foreground. The significance of such compositions has been discussed in Chapter 4. This photograph is superimposed over a picture of Knocknarea, which is also viewed from a distance and framed by foliage. The mountain is slightly obscured by mist, connoting a mythical landscape only partly located in the real world, which may vanish at any time. The use of mist to signify mythical or magical places and figures (such as wraiths, fairies and spirits) is an established motif in a variety of media, especially film, television and theatre. It usually presages the arrival of a mystical creature, such as the witches on the moors in Macbeth, Herne the Hunter in the Tales of Robin Hood or the Lady of the Lake in King Arthur and the Knights of the Round Table. Three photographs representing the facilities of the hotel (dining room, bedroom, games room) are placed below the main picture.

The brochure was folded twice to open out in two sections. The first section introduces the location of the product in lyrical language, in a cursive font (Figure 5.13). The text begins with the endorsement of W. B. Yeats, Ireland's first Nobel Laureate, who 'often spoke of Sligo and its surrounding country as his first home, his first love'; a painting of Yeats is included as corroboration. An implicit invitation to 'indulg[e] in the wonders of this land of hearts (*sic*) desire' is accompanied by photographs of these 'wonders': 'majestic Ben Bulben', 'Queen Maeve's Knocknarea', a Celtic high cross, and, to bring back to mind the hotel amongst all of these historical and mythical place images, a garden flower arrangement on a polished wooden table, placed directly underneath the word 'guest'.

Having established the mood of the place, a magical land where 'friends are made and memories are golden!', the brochure opens out into the second section where the text continues in the same vein as the previous section, 'A land rich in history, spoilt with the choice of natures (*sic*) finest, a people lyrical in language and generous in spirit'. This flows into a description of the hotel, in the same short statements, 'Warm glowing fires, grande cuisine prepared by creative hands: fine wines from around the world ...'. In this way, it is unclear where the description of the place ends and that of the hotel begins; the hotel become part of the place image. The photographs in this section present the facilities in the hotel and the activities available locally. Their size and positioning in relation to the text reflect those in the previous section, reinforcing the equation of the product with the place. The theme of a fantastical place is carried through the hotel description, where 'The experience is everything', there is 'so much to see, so much to do ... a paradise of choice' in 'a unique atmosphere in a world of modern banality', and visitors are 'welcome[d] to a gentle peace'.

Given the limited budget, this brochure was the main promotional tool used by the business in establishing an identity and, as such, a conscious decision was made by the management 'to sell an image rather than listing facilities'. The juxtaposition of product and place photographs, combined with the way in which the written text draws the reader into the place (a fantastic, imaginary image of the place), then into the product, manages to equate the product with this mythical land. The message conveyed is that by staying in this hotel, the reader can visit this magical realm themselves. Once the mood is established, a more comprehensive list of facilities available in the hotel and locally can be included in a separate letter in mail shots, for example.

Figure 5.13 First section of brochure of Business B

Both of these businesses, to varying extents, attempted to tap into an established image of County Sligo, one particularly present in the literary tradition of W. B. Yeats. This mythical land was invoked through explicit references to 'the land of hearts desire' and the Yeats country, as well as the use of mythological motifs such as: Knocknarea, the site of Miscaun Maeve, a passage tomb reputed to be the grave of the mythical Queen Maeve of Connacht; the megalithic cemetery of

Carrowmore, two miles south-west of Sligo town, said to be the last resting place of the defeated Fir Bolg (another mythological race identified in *Lebor Gabála Érenn* (Ó Cuív, 1968) who invaded Ireland before the Tuatha Dé Danann); and Ben Bulben, where the mythical figure of Diarmuid, a member of the Fiana who had wandered Ireland with his beloved Gráinne in fear of pursuit by Fionn mac Cumhaill (leader of the Fiana and Gráinne's betrothed) is said to have died (Kalogara, 1977; Kilgannon, 1989). Examples such as these highlight the ways in which the symbolic meanings of place can be tapped into in product promotion.

Notes

1 The Book of Kells is a vellum manuscript dating from c. 800 AD and contains a Latin text of the four Gospels in insular majuscule script accompanied by intricate whole pages of decoration with smaller painted decorations appearing throughout the text. It is the most elaborate manuscript of its kind to survive from the early Middle Ages and is permanently on display in the Library of Trinity College Dublin.

2 The term "Gaeltacht" describes those areas in the Republic of Ireland where the Irish language is the community language. The Gaeltacht covers extensive parts of counties Donegal, Galway, Kerry and Mayo, all of which are on the western seaboard, together with parts of counties Cork, Meath and Waterford.

Chapter 6

The Adaptation and Use of Existing Images in Place Promotion

> Places have become commodities to be packaged, marketed and sold … Contemporary media, especially television, play a powerful ideological role in "mapping" the social and cultural characteristics of different places (Burgess, 1985) … [and] myth is more important than reality in selling places (Burgess and Wood, 1988, p. 94).

Place image promotion rarely occurs in a vacuum (Ashworth and Voogd, 1994). More often, it involves adapting to, altering or making use of existing images, which are drawn from a multiplicity of sources over which the place marketer has little influence. In relation to tourism promotion, Mellinger (1994) summarizes succinctly the multiple influences on the modern tourist's expectations.

> Tourists inhabit a mass-mediated culture in which the proliferation of hegemonically-scripted discourses, including television programs, feature films, travel books, brochures, and postcards, act as powerful tour guides that can produce ideals, identities, and role models for tourists, and define their situations, set their agendas, and establish the boundaries of their gaze (p. 776).

This provides challenges for place promoters because, as Burgess (1982) observes, organizations and individuals involved in the business of promoting places have to try to emphasize the positive imagery which already exists about the place whilst simultaneously challenging unfavourable images.

In the sample of promotional materials under investigation here, this adaptation and exploitation of existing images was very much the case with the same well-known images being used again and again (Clonmacnoise, River Shannon, Ring of Kerry, Bantry Bay, Dingle Peninsula), and the overall images portrayed of the three study regions (rural, beautiful scenery, heritage attractions, friendly people, opportunities for recreational activities), as identified in the previous chapter, broadly matching the image being portrayed by Bord Fáilte of the country as a whole (Prentice and Andersen, 2000). Many respondents, particularly craftspeople, also used images of Ireland and "Irishness" to tap into positive imagery that exists of the country world-wide. In this chapter I will explore some of these findings and examine several of the images of Ireland which have been identified in academic research in order to compare and contrast the findings of the current study with these descriptions.

I will begin, however, with a particularly good example from the promotional literature of an image adapting and making use of existing images of a place. The image is a golf club logo, similar to the one discussed in the preceding chapter. As with the previous logo, the traditional heraldic sign format is used which again symbolizes tradition, longevity and nobility. The second logo also uses graphic place images, again, those connected with the sea (deep blue water, a ship and islands), but also imagery specifically associated with County Kerry (Figure 6.1).

Figure 6.1 Crest logo 2 (business name removed)

The islands represent the Blaskets, three islands located off the coast of Kerry. The Blaskets as a symbolic landscape embody a variety of myths, many associated with the rich literary tradition of the islands and particularly with the famous biography, *Peig* (Ní Mhainnín and Ó Mhurchú, 1998). Based on the stories of Peig Sayers, a native of the islands, this text was a staple of the Irish secondary school syllabus until the mid-1990s and the imagery associated with this book has become embedded in the Irish cultural psyche. A variety of images connote a traditional Irish culture, the Irish language and the myths associated with an island community surviving in a harsh environment. Another element of the sign which has Kerry associations is the ship. As well as being an index of the sea, the ship could be representative of Viking long-ships which invaded Ireland at the end of the eighth century. However, the symbol of the cross on the sails indicates that it represents St. Brendan the Navigator, the best know of this county's saints. Mount Brandon is usually held to have been named after him. On Brendan's famous voyage in search of a paradise island in the western ocean, a survival of pagan belief, he is said to have discovered America. The ninth century Latin account of this voyage is probably Ireland's single greatest contribution to European medieval literature and it is said to have inspired Columbus (Barrington, 1976). The grey castle denotes an actual place on the golf course, the Barrow Castle, which is a late 13th century stone castle built by either the Fitz Maurices or the de Clahull family (Barrington, 1976). However, it is its connotative meanings which have most significance, representing an ancient heritage, history and, in using the same colour grey as the islands, associating with traditional Irish culture and landscape. The denotation of an elevated golfing green is more explicit than in the previous logo, with the red pin marking the golf hole. The yellow denotes a sand bunker, but is also a metonym for a links golf course and again evokes coastal landscape imagery. The crossed golf clubs are similar to those discussed in relation to the previous logo (reminiscent of the crossed swords symbol often used on heraldic signs), while the red rose, in addition to being a symbol sometimes used on crests, represents the famous Rose of Tralee Festival, which draws on a local, well-known romantic legend and has become one of the most famous festivals and beauty pageants in the country.

In relation to existing images of Ireland, in early literature and tradition, certain images were associated with particular regions. The four provinces of the country were characterized in different ways: the East (Leinster) by wealth and prosperity, the South (Munster) by music and traditional crafts, the West (Connacht) by learning and history, and the North (Ulster) by conflict and war (Kockel, 1995). These images are based on a text written in Middle Irish dating from circa AD 550 and are somewhat out-dated, with the provincial divisions now functioning principally in the organization of sporting events. Kockel (1995) sees the predominant regional images of Ireland today as being those of the North and the West. The West's image is one of a place apart, a haven from modern industrialized society, whilst the Northern image is one of conflict and war, and questions of identity are bound up in the Catholic/Protestant, Nationalist/Unionist dichotomy (Connolly, 1997; Poole, 1997). Northern Ireland poses a particular problem in relation to regional imagery, especially vis-à-vis place promotion. As already noted, tourism or place promotion does not occur in a vacuum and images of a region or country are portrayed in many different ways through media, film and books. Until very recently, Northern Ireland was only portrayed in the world media when violence occurred or when something related took place in a particular country, e.g. the extradition of a prisoner. Therefore, these are the images of the region to which the potential tourist market was being exposed (Rolston, 1995).

The organizations and producers I surveyed tended to agree with Kockel's (1995) assessment of the predominance of regional images of the North and West of Ireland. When asked how it was felt consumers viewed the regions, many, particularly in the Northwest, spoke of 'the troubles in the North'. One organizational respondent stated that 'at all stages we need to portray an image of a peaceful and tranquil [product] because, for example, in the U.S., people think that Connemara is in Northern Ireland'. At the same time, a significant proportion of producers in the Midlands felt that the West of Ireland was the only place known to tourists: 'The image of the West, Southwest and Northwest is so strong, that this part of the world doesn't get a look in', 'People don't think of the Midlands, people think of Ireland as Kerry, Cork and so on', 'Look up any [web]site, any Bord Fáilte book, you only see tourist areas – Kerry, Killarney, Clare'. One organization in the Northwest highlighted the fact that tourism businesses in Roscommon 'use images of the West of Ireland rather than the Midlands' because these images are more likely to sell their product.

As identified by many commentators (Byrne *et al.*, 1993; Kockel, 1995; Gibbons, 1996; Duffy, 1997; Kneafsey, 1997), the West of Ireland, including the south-west and north-west, retains a romantic image of a magical place apart, a place in sharp contrast to urbanized, industrial life where the traditional Irish culture and way of life survives. The West as the site of true Irishness was constructed historically in two ways: by English colonists in the seventeenth and eighteenth centuries to whom it represented the "primitive other" (Kneafsey, 1997), and by the early 20th century literary revivalists and the Irish-Ireland movement who saw the West of Ireland as the last remaining outpost of true Irishness (Nash, 1993). Since the collision of the Gaelic and English cultures in the 16th century, Ireland's identity has been constructed historically in terms of the "colonial other". Over time, as the rest of the country became corrupted by anglicization and urbanization, the West came to serve as a primitive "Other" against which the pre-eminence of the colonial power could be gauged (Nash, 1993).

'National memory is an important aspect of national identity' (Azaryahu and Kellerman, 1999, p. 109) and revivalism as a cultural convention played an important part in defining Irish identity in the late nineteenth century, influencing a number of different fields: linguistic, educational, literary, religious, political and artistic. Douglas Hyde, the first president of Ireland, was one of the founders of the Gaelic League and argued for the de-anglicization of Irish culture and the restoration of ancient Gaelic traditions and language. Padraig Pearse criticized the education system in Ireland for censoring Irish national heritage by prohibiting the playing of Gaelic games, the speaking of the native language and the teaching of the "true history" of Irish people (Kearney, 1988). Within the Anglo-Irish literary revival, William Butler Yeats, George Russell and Lady Gregory proposed that 'Ireland could only be redeemed from the prevailing spiritlessness of modernity ... by retrieving the myths of the Celtic past ... [and] by restoring a sense of spiritual continuity with the past' (Kearney, 1988, p. 11). The founding of the Abbey Theatre was a means of reliving this ancient Celtic heritage and reviving Celtic mythology so that Irish culture could reclaim its rightful identity. This harking back to tradition was also endorsed by nationalist elements within the Irish Catholic Church and by the Irish Republican movement of 1916 (Kearney, 1988).

'The shaping of landscape can reflect and reinforce ideas of what constitutes a people, who is included, or excluded' (Crang, 1998, p. 40). Within nationalist ideology, the rock-strewn, barren landscape of the West of Ireland came to symbolize Ireland as a whole in opposition to the 18th century estate landscapes which were seen to represent English exploitation of Ireland (Graham, 1997). Duncan (1990) suggests that a cultural landscape is a collection of images which sum up a people's vision of itself and helps to define a collective identity. The establishment of the West of Ireland landscape as the cultural heartland of the country played a fundamental role in the formation of Irish nationalism as 'the creation of hegemonic landscape narratives ... denot[es] particular places as centres of collective cultural consciousness' (Graham, 1997, p. 7). The idealized, unspoilt landscape of the West, untouched by modernity, came to represent Ireland before suppression by England. Identity is often defined in distinction from a hostile "Other" (Said, 1993) and the West's "Otherness" from England and the estate landscapes elsewhere in Ireland contributed to its elevation to the quintessential Irish landscape.

Such images of the West were further elaborated in the era of film (Duffy, 1997).

> Robert O'Flaherty's *Man of Aran* (1934) is a cinematic reflection of the theme of wild beauty in the western isle. In *The Quiet Man* (1952) John Ford celebrates the West as a passionate, patriarchal, violent society, while David Lean's *Ryan's Daughter* (1970) and Jim Sheridan's *The Field* (1992) can be seen as more recent manifestations of this self-same mythology (p. 68).

The "real" Ireland of the revivalists was a rural Ireland, a myth created by artists, intellectuals and political leaders, such as William Butler and Jack Yeats, Paul Henry, Sean Keating, George Russell, Michael Collins and Eamon de Valera, who themselves were the urban based descendants of country people (Gibbons, 1996; Kiberd, 1996). Revivalist literature and opinion portrayed the rural as a romantic idyll where the traditions of true Ireland persisted, and the farmer as the moral and economic backbone of the country. In a famous radio broadcast at the height of his power, de Valera's 'rural idyll … – "the contests of athletic youth … the laughter of comely maidens … the wisdom of old age in the chimney corner …" and so on' gives an indication of this romantic view (de Paor, 1979, p. 354).

The idealization of the West and the equation of rurality with true Irishness has also been a dominant theme in 20th century Irish art (Gibbons, 1996). In fact, as Duffy (1997) notes, Paul Henry's depictions of 20th century Achill's 'desolate landscapes of thatched houses and blue mountains became part of the nationalist iconography of the Free State' (p. 67). Even prior to this, rural Ireland was portrayed by most artists in terms of wild, romantic, picturesque landscapes, with little reference to the reality of social and economic conditions of the time (Brett, 1994; Duffy, 1994). As early as 1841, travel writers wrote of the romanticized landscape of the West of Ireland and the peasant as a 'valuable accessory to the landscape' (Hall and Hall, 1841 quoted in Brett, 1994, p. 123).

A sentimental, static and conservative view of rurality was set up in opposition to modernity and informed the political ideology of the new Irish Free State. The dominance of rural themes in Irish literature continued throughout the 20th century, strengthening the clichéd representation of Ireland as a rural place and feeding into the rural nostalgia which survives today (Duffy, 1997). This myth of an essentially rural Ireland in need of protection from Yeats' 'filthy modern tide' has been charged with stifling development and modernization in Ireland under de Valera's leadership (Kockel, 1995). An idealistic view of rurality existed so much so that writers such as Synge were accused of misrepresenting Irish rural life, yet those who objected to *The Playboy of the Western World*[1] in 1907 were urban people who saw rurality as their heritage and choose to view it in soft focus. When the play was shown in the West of Ireland, it was seen as unremarkable (Kiberd, 1996).

The myth of the West is not only an Irish phenomenon.

> The invocation of the west as the source of heroism, mystery and romance … is found in many different cultures under such varied names as Atlantis, Elysium, El Dorado or the English Land of Cockaigne (Gibbons, 1996, p. 23).

Gibbons (1996) compares the western myth in Ireland to that of the American West. Both are seen as places where traditional cultures and values have survived, untouched by modernization. This appeals to counter-culturally inclined immigrants who, since the late 1960s, have settled on the west coast of Ireland. Not only is Celtic imagery part of the New Age symbolism, but this movement also contends that things are done differently in the West and that there is a more informal regional economy than elsewhere in the developed world (Kockel, 1995).

Historically, the idyllic view of the countryside was accompanied by the image of a 'rustic, ahistorical and apolitical community life … where timeless quaint characters go about their humble and picturesque ways' (Leerssen, 1996, p. 170). Whereas in England, the archetype of the Stage Irishman was a malevolent and unappealing caricature, the primitive "Other", to the early 20th century revivalists and nationalists the Irish peasant was rural, Gaelic, Catholic, poor, yet pure in soul and body and representing a peasantry wisdom (Kockel, 1995). Although such images have little relevance in modern Ireland, they may still have some currency among the Irish diaspora.

> Because the meanings of identity spaces are undergoing continual renegotiations, disjunctions often occur in which … contemporary diasporic versions of national allegiance remain sited in past circumstances that pay little heed to the ongoing evolution of identity in the metropolitan state (Graham, 2000, p. 72).

Nash (1993) observes that images of the West of Ireland continue to be used today in tourism promotion as a representation of the landscape of Ireland as a whole, whilst O'Connor (1993) contends that images used by tourist organizations tap into pre-existing stereotypes, selecting some of the more benign supposed characteristics of Ireland and Irish people to promote the country abroad.

Academic study of contemporary regional images in Ireland is of relatively recent origin and readily available studies relate in particular to links with the promotion of Ireland as a tourism destination. The evolution of Irish tourism promotion is grounded in the fact that historically Ireland has been dependent on the British and the U.S. tourist markets. Whilst tourist images are created to combine the needs of the tourist with what the host country has to offer, they are also selected from a range of images already in existence in the market countries. These images evolved, in Britain, from colonial rule (an unpopulated landscape; virgin territory to be claimed by the tourist) and, in the U.S., from the vast numbers of Irish émigrés (Ireland is a fictional land where time has stood still and the landscape is unchanged and unspoiled; it is a Tír na nÓg,[2] where tourists can come to rejuvenate themselves) (O'Connor, 1993). Johnson (2000) uses the terms 'empty space' and 'empty time' to describe these representations of Ireland. In Britain and the U.S. there is extensive imagery to tap into, but in other markets, e.g. Italy, the images of Ireland are more limited. However, O'Connor (1993) identifies a number of common themes that continue to be reproduced for tourist consumption. These include the image of Ireland as a picturesque, unspoiled, timeless country with a friendly and quaint people, and a place where past traditions and ways of life still exist, in other words, a pre-modern society. As already mentioned, traditional stereotypes have been tapped into so that, for example, an image of laziness becomes a positive attribute in terms of a laid-back society, where nobody is rushed and tourists can relax. Where work is represented, it is romanticized and portrayed in terms of people working with the land or as skilled, traditional craftwork. Other images relate to a friendly and hospitable people, timelessness, where visitors are released from their everyday constraints of time, and the beautiful, unpolluted landscape.

These traditional images of Ireland as unpopulated landscape and a place where time has stood still can be found in abundance in the promotional literature examined here. As discussed in the previous chapter, one organizational respondent stated that they deliberately left excess people out of landscape photographs in order to depict a secluded, unpopulated countryside, but without being too barren, so 'so we show people as well'. Also, few of the scenic shots in the producers' sample of promotional materials contained more than one or two people. The slogans, particularly in the Midlands, encouraged tourists to explore and discover: '*Explore the Shannon…*', '*Voyage of Discovery*'. Written text referred to the unspoiled nature of the environment and the tranquillity and peace to be found: 'a place for peace and contemplation', 'a beautiful and tranquil environment'.

The Ireland of the fictional land frozen in time was evident in the crafts producers' promotional materials, through links between rurality and authenticity, and traditional skills in opposition to modern, industrial production (Figures 4.1 and 5.1). Slogans claimed there was '*History in the making*' and products represented '*Ireland… past and present*'. In this fictional land, the traditions of 'the ancient crafts' were 'often handed down from father to son'. In the promotional literature of tourism respondents, the absence of markers of modernity, explicit references to stepping back in time, and the construction of symbolic places which are havens from modern, industrial life have been discussed (see Chapter 5).

As indicated, Nash (1993) contends that the West of Ireland landscape is used in national and international tourism promotion as a representation of Ireland as a whole. The image of the West has been constructed 'as both representative and different, its difference lying in its offer to the tourist of unique access to true Irishness' (Nash, 1993, p. 87). Kneafsey (1997) supports this contention in her examination of promotional materials relating to County Mayo, with brochures asserting that 'Mayo is the most Irish part of Ireland' (p. 150). The overall themes emerging from all the representations and texts of Mayo examined include: coastal scenery, mountains/wilderness/rural scenery, historical ruins, holiday activities, traditions/music, and people/history/legend.

These themes broadly match those identified by Quinn, B. (1994) in her content analysis of verbal and visual presentations in brochures produced to promote Ireland as a tourist destination in Continental Europe. She identified a number of broad concepts: a world apart from modern society, an attractive, unspoiled environment, friendly people, a relaxed pace of life, a vast cultural heritage, and a large selection of sporting opportunities. The actual images incorporating these themes included: mostly rural landscapes, vernacular (thatched cottages, stone walls) and spectacular (castles, mansions) architecture, people in traditional attire and carrying out traditional activities (bringing home the hay), aspects of historical legacy (Celtic crosses), and the natural environment as a location for sporting activities (golf, angling). She notes that 'Any semblance of "modern life", instantly familiar to the predominantly urbanized Europeans targeted by the brochures is carefully disguised' (p. 65). Quinn, B. (1994) speculates that this may be detrimental to other areas of Irish life: political, economic, cultural, and that an increasingly sophisticated tourist market will not be attracted by a singular emphasis on Ireland's rurality.

In looking at images of Connemara in the West of Ireland, Byrne *et al.* (1993) state that '"Connemara" as perceived from one social vantage point or another is a construct which is assembled out of different components, depending partly on the requirements of the viewer' (p. 236). Different images of the area that are identified include: a magical, peripheral area, the last outpost of true Irishness, and a refuge or contrast from modern urbanized life. Connemara has long been described as authentic, but various versions of authenticity can be identified, from its depiction as the location of unpolluted Irishness postulated by the revivalists, to its designation as a place of escape from modernization, the last frontier identified by Synge (Byrne *et al.*, 1993).

Bell (1995) defines images of the Irish landscape in terms of their portrayal in photographs and text in the promotional literature used to market Ireland in the German tourist market. These representations of the landscape have borrowed heavily from artistic representations and produce an image of Ireland as a romantic tourist destination. This image is placed within a framework of a set of visual codes and literary sensibilities, already present in the popular culture of a particular class of German tourist. These are partly derived from a long-established travel and ethnographic literature relating to Ireland, but also draw from a more general discourse present in German popular visual culture which has its roots in a northern Romantic landscape artistic tradition. This provides 'a "perfect frame" for the German experience of Ireland' (Bell, 1995, p. 49).

These various images of the West of Ireland as identified in the literature (a magical place apart, an authentic place, a haven from modern society, the last outpost of true Irishness) were definitely utilized in promoting the products of both crafts and tourism businesses in the Northwest and Southwest, from the thatched cottage logo (Figure 5.1) and its connotations, to the many textual references to location; 'Idyllically set at the head of Bantry Bay', 'the most westerly [product] in Europe', 'untouched by the industrial revolution … full of history and legend …

lush green countryside', 'His work ... evokes all that is the West of Ireland'. Sligo was portrayed by some producers, particularly artists and the two tourism case studies highlighted in the previous chapter, as a magical place apart, although not necessarily peripheral. Rural Ireland as the "real" Ireland of the early revivalists was also evident in the sample. The images in both the organizations' and producers' literature were overwhelmingly drawn from rural landscapes, and when asked what images they were trying to convey, organizational responses were remarkably similar: 'rural nature', 'unspoiled', 'we use rural images, the beauty of the landscape', 'a rustic, quiet, people-friendly place'. Very few urban images existed and some organizations said that they deliberately did not choose urban or industrial imagery for promotional purposes: 'we don't draw attention to them [referring to chemical plants in the region]', 'we wouldn't sell the urban aspect'.

One of the myths of the West, that of its position as the last bastion of true Irishness, was being challenged by those in the Midlands. Respondents in this region argued that the West had become overrun with tourists and was no longer authentically Irish. It was stated that the Midlands 'still has a natural environment and ordinary local people', unlike the "hyperreality" of many places in the West of Ireland, where the tourist will meet only other tourists. They also argued that the service and product in the Midlands are still authentic, and not simply 'put on for the tourist' as they are in the West, or, in MacCannell's (1976, pp. 91-107) words, not a 'staged authenticity'. Organizations and producers in the Midlands were attempting to position the region as the 'real Ireland' or the 'heart of [modern] Ireland'. Slogans stated '*It's Central, It's Special*', '*in the heart of Ireland*' and textual references to its ideal situation in 'the heart of Ireland', 'the centre of Ireland' and 'the crossroads of Ireland' abounded.

To a large extent many of the themes identified by O'Connor (1993), Kneafsey (1997) and Quinn, B. (1994) were found in the current sample of both crafts and tourism respondents' literature. Certainly, Ireland as picturesque and attractive was evident in photographs (Figures 4.1, 4.2, 4.3, 4.4, 5.4, 5.7, 5.8, 5.9 and 5.10), logos (Figures 5.3 and 6.1), and written text (numerous references to beautiful scenery). The various scenic images identified by Kneafsey (1997) were present in large quantities in the sample, particularly in the Northwest and Southwest. Coastal imagery was primarily shown in the Southwest for both tourism and crafts, but also in the Northwest, for tourism mainly. Similarly mountains and wilderness were mostly present in the Northwest for tourism, but also in the Southwest for both products. Images of rural scenery were present in the three regions and, as identified, urban imagery was lacking. The unspoiled environment was implicit in many of the logos which used flowers, vegetation, greenery and animals (Figure 5.2), and in landscape photographs and those illustrating various outdoor activities (such as Figures 5.4 and 5.5). Numerous textual references were made to the unspoiled natural environment, particularly in the promotional literature of tourism respondents.

In the tourism promotional literature, the image of friendly people was apparent in photographs of hospitable owners and enthusiastic staff, with smiling, welcoming faces denoting "homeliness" and a quality service (see Chapter 4 for a more detailed account). Also, textual references to the proprietors as managers of the property ensured personal service and attention, and declarations of hospitality ('the farmhouse with a thousand welcomes') and customer care ('[Name of owners] insist on the utmost comfort for all their guests') contributed to this image. In relation to crafts products, photographs of happy, smiling people were used to represent satisfied consumers.

Another frequently occurring theme in photographs was that of people engaged in the activity of the business, in other words, playing golf, fishing, sailing, boating or dining, as well as people engaged in other activities, usually those available locally such as horse riding, walking and visiting local attractions. According to Briggs (1997) it is useful to use photographs of people having fun or carrying out suitable activities in tourism promotion, particularly if the people look like the target market. Figure 6.2 illustrates a typical example of a photograph used to promote angling businesses.

Figure 6.2 Photograph of a fisherman

Once again, the photograph as proof of the event comes into play using some simple iconic codes. The semes included in this composition include: a smiling man posing for the camera with a fish held in his hands in a gesture of display; a net full of similar fish; plastic containers and various pieces of half unseen equipment; and, a body of water surrounded by green vegetation. These various signifiers combine to produce a syntagmatic composition of a seasoned (well-equipped) angler, satisfied (smiling) and proud (displaying his catch for the camera) after a highly successful fishing trip (numerous fish in the net positioned at his feet, implying the entire catch is his). The green vegetation in the background symbolizes an unspoiled and fertile environment, a theme reflected in the multitude of clean fish in the net. As noted above, photographs are most successful in tourism marketing when they show people having fun or partaking of appropriate activities, particularly if they look like the target market (Briggs, 1997). This principle has been adhered to in the majority of the photographs present in the sample, as it is here, as the target consumer for angling businesses in Ireland is generally male, aged over 35 years (the man in the picture) and in the ABC1 social class, i.e. managerial/professional/ white collar, and so could afford the expensive equipment shown (Bord Fáilte, 1997). The intended reader is expected to identify with the angler and believe that he too can be this successful if he visits this area. This is a good example of the denoted message (a smiling man with fishing equipment displaying a fish and a full net) naturalizing the symbolic message (satisfaction and success guaranteed).

All of the photographs of people engaged in various activities employ similar methods to connote comparable messages. There was a preponderance of photographs of males, either alone or in groups, in the Midlands and Northwest, whilst photographs of children only slightly outnumbered those of males, in the Southwest. The majority of these photographs were of men engaged in traditional male activities, in particular golf and fishing. Photographs of females were more varied, but were generally of women engaged in more passive activities, such as: sitting in a garden, on a bed, inside a barge, in a sauna; enjoying a massage and other health farm activities; and, viewing various attractions. In the entire sample, there were only two photographs of women playing golf and two of women cycling. In the Midlands and Northwest, photographs containing children depicted open farms, horse riding, pets and a playground. In the Southwest, most photographs were of children engaged in various water sports. All were present in the promotional literature of one respondent who specialized in these types of activity holidays. Photographs of couples, families and mixed gender groups depicted a variety of active and passive recreations, including boating, dining, walking, hiking, cycling, swimming and open farms.

Notwithstanding this prevalence of images of friendly people in the promotional materials examined, the quaintness identified by O'Connor (1993) and the people in traditional attire highlighted by Quinn, B. (1994) were not in evidence. People were shown in modern clothes and emphasis was placed on a friendly, efficient, quality service with personal attention. However, the relaxing pace of life was evident in the theme of "tranquillity" and getting away from the stresses of modern life and the themes of timelessness and a world apart from modern society have been discussed. Quinn, B.'s (1994) finding that modernity was disguised was reflected to a certain extent in the present sample, in that emphasis was not placed on modernity. However, as mentioned, modern clothes were shown and modern conveniences highlighted (lists of local services; references to proximity to local towns with services). Modernity was not hidden, but attention was not drawn to it.

Frequent textual references to the 'craic' to be had and traditional Irish music in pubs, as well as invitations to 'Step over the threshold and take a step back in time' to 'the old fashioned comfort of...', portrayed an image of a place where past traditions and ways of life exist. These themes were also evident in crafts producers' literature where an emphasis was placed on traditional, handmade methods of production, handed down from generation to generation or the 'the age-old tradition of the Celt'.

Similar motifs were identified in the textual imagery relating to the theme of "craftsmanship and tradition" in the three regions. This theme was most prevalent in the Southwest and descriptions of the product as being handmade were the most frequently occurring motif in this region: 'because all the [product] produced is absolutely hand made, the spirit of the crafts man is liberated, unencumbered by machines of mass production'. The secondary meaning plainly connotes the myth of the handmade craft as authentic and binarily opposed to modern (artificial), industrial based production. This premise was also echoed in the other two regions. In the Midlands, handmade production was correlated with uniqueness, individuality and integrity: 'each uniquely handcrafted item ... the individual piece'; 'there is a feeling of hands being on each piece ... we take tremendous pride in the integrity of our material and in the imaginative way we fashion it'. Similarly, in the Northwest, the craftworker referred to handmade production as a deliberate choice: 'I like to work [raw material] by hand because it creates the opportunity to develop a special relationship with the material and subject matter'. By implication, other manufactured products are insincere and contrived.

Within this category in the Midlands, various eloquent references to the craftsmanship and skill of the craftworker were the most commonly occurring motif. Examples included: '[the craft] is a highly skilled operation which requires both natural aptitude and meticulous training'; 'his handling of paint is wonderfully sensitive'; 'its beauty is now revealed by the hand of the sculptor'. Such images were also common in the Southwest, but less so in the Northwest, although the descriptive rhetoric was remarkably similar in the three regions: 'the final forms are vested with the skill and artistry of the Master Craftsman' (Northwest); 'in the sensitive hands of [craftsperson] they reappear in an infinite variety of elegant and enchanting forms' (Southwest). Such descriptions evoke images of creativity, artistic flair and originality. Here, the line is blurred between crafts production and fine art.

In the Northwest, references to the professional history of the producer, in terms of listings of previous exhibitions, qualifications and experience, occurred most often in the "craftsmanship and tradition" category, followed closely by accounts of the various methods of production used. Whilst such practical details were also used in the other two regions, their predominance in the Northwest may relate to the fact that many of these craft businesses were relatively new (35 percent were in operation for five years or less). Many businesses were, therefore, still at the market penetration stage, where product differentiation and establishing a reputation were most important. Consumers and customers were likely to be in the early stages of the product adoption process and seeking information about the product's features, uses, advantages and distinctions (Dibb *et al.*, 1991). The fact that the "product characteristics/praise" theme ranked higher in this region than in the Midlands or Southwest supports this notion. Descriptive statements in praise of the product, ‘Our [products] are a joy to send to our friends’, references to its uniqueness, ‘each design is truly unique, a piece of art’, and assurances of quality, ‘We have used only the best quality [raw material]’, were the techniques used to constitute this theme. Again, the objectives of product distinction, reputation building and positive image creation are clear. Textual descriptions in both of these categories demonstrated some of the elements used in product differentiation (Kotler, 1997), namely, product features and performance (methods of production, raw materials used, professional history of the craftworker), reliability (long tradition of craftwork, assurances of quality) and style and design (product praise, artistic qualities). Very few photographs fell into this “product characteristics/praise” category. Those which did mostly portrayed the track record of the product in terms of being used in award ceremonies and presentations.

In relation to O’Connor’s (1993) assertion that, where work was represented, it was romanticized, in the tourism literature of the present study, there were very few images of work. Those portrayed were primarily of hotel staff carrying out their duties, albeit with a smile on their faces and accompanied by text such as ‘From the moment you arrive we are ever-mindful of your individual desires, and are unwavering in our resolve to fulfil them to your satisfaction’, connoting a welcoming, willing personal service. In crafts, however, work was idealized, with craftspeople shown in solitary work, working with their hands and so immersed in their work that they are unaware of the camera.

Figure 6.3 Craftsperson at work (craftsperson’s face blurred)

The majority of these photographs fell into the “craftsmanship and tradition” theme identified above and showed the craftsperson at work, the craftsperson’s tools and the craftsperson with the product or alone. These photographs provide evidence that the products are handmade by a real person. The semes in these iconic codes are: a person sitting or standing at a workbench not directly facing the reader; casual, work-like clothing (sometimes an apron); small objects which can be identified as various types of tools either in the hands of, or next to, the person; the product in an unfinished state (usually being handled by the person); a room containing other unfinished products, raw materials and work benches. The iconographic code at work in these compositions combines all of these signified elements to signify a craftsperson creating a product by hand, so engrossed in their work that they are oblivious of the gaze of the reader (Figure 6.3).

Photographs of the tools used by craftworkers employ the myth of the photograph capturing the past to connote their meaning (Figure 6.4).

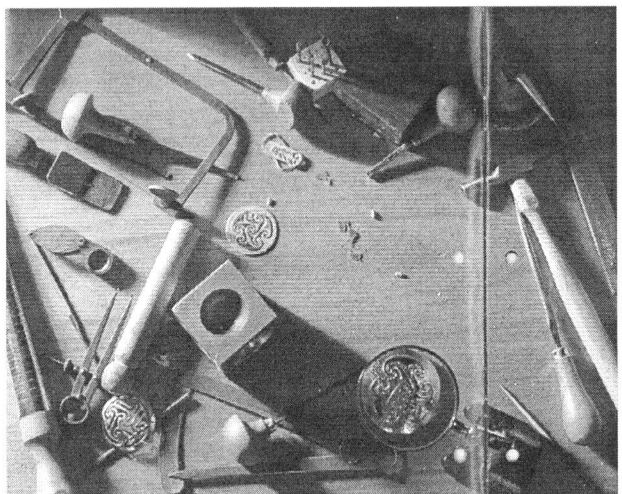

Figure 6.4 Craftworker's tools

The paradigmatic choice of the positioning of the tools is significant. They are not laid out clean and tidy ready to be used or put away in a box or on a shelf, all of which are images which could have been chosen. The meaning signified by the image of the tools in disarray is that the craftworker has just finished making the product for you, the reader, and that exact moment in time has been captured by the camera. The soft lighting and use of shadows imply that the sun is setting, so the craftworker has finished for the day, but the tools have been left to resume in the morning. The notions of the continuity of the craftwork over time and the craft as organic and continually developing, as opposed to stagnant and unchanging, are signified. The fact that samples of the product are still present adds to the sense of work being continued. This is an example of codes of taste and sensibility establishing these particular connotations in this situation; in another setting and with different lighting and compositional effects, these tools in disarray could connote confusion, disorder or panic.

Of the other imagery identified in the literature, historical ruins were very much evident in the Northwest and Midlands, in tourism promotional materials. Whilst such images were apparent in the Southwest in the tourism literature, they were more prevalent in the crafts producers' materials, particularly in the promotional media of one crafts producer who provides another useful case study of the successful use of place imagery in practice.

As we saw in the previous chapter, Business B was a good example of the way in which one piece of promotional material can be used successfully to create an image of product and place. By way of contrast, a number of businesses in the Southwest used some of the greatest variety of media. The case in question here (Business C) used the Irish language and legends, regional landscapes and local historical and archaeological features both in product design and promotion in a very conscious and co-ordinated way. Several different reasons were identified for the use of this strategy, but with the one intention of positioning the product as the embodiment of Irish culture in order to target a mainly tourist and foreign market. This business was established 18 years prior to the interview in a Gaeltacht area in Kerry. The producer had trained in the craft he practiced and had worked abroad for a number of years. He wished to return to west Kerry where he had family connections, and did so when he identified a niche in the market for his particular product; nobody else was producing it in the area at the time. He received capital assistance from Údarás na Gaeltachta (a Regional Development Agency with responsibility for the economic, social and cultural development of the Gaeltacht regions), as well as technical assistance to receive further specialized training in the particular type of craft product he wished to produce. The business grew from a family operated enterprise to employing 12 full-time and eight seasonal staff.

The product consisted of a wide range of handmade, batch gift items and the unique selling point was the use of local and Irish imagery in product design. Different ranges of the product were given Gaelic/cultural titles, such as the Newgrange, Cashel, Tara, Ogham Stone, Durrow, Aisling, Clonfert, Ardfert, Tullylease, Shannon, Lir, Celtic Cross and Celtic Spirals Collections, as well as individually titled pieces such as the Kells, Kinnitty, Aran, Inisfree, Oisín, Setanta and Shamrock pieces.

The initial marketing of the product was very simple. The producer bought a premises and set up a small workshop in the back and sold what he produced in the front. The shop was of an open plan design, so consumers could watch the craftworker producing the product. This became a tourist attraction and boosted sales. The theme of watching the craftsman at work continued throughout the promotional materials eventually developed. As the business grew, the workshop was moved out of the shop to an Údarás subsidized factory unit and apprentices were employed. The respondent started selling wholesale and marketed the products to retailers through direct personal contact, attendance at trade shows in Ireland and abroad and advertising in trade magazines. He also opened two more retail outlets. The enterprise moved to a larger Údarás building as it continued to expand and, at the time of interview, the owner was negotiating to buy the premises outright. As well as advertising to the trade, local cinema, magazines and the Aer Lingus in-flight magazine, *Cara*, were used to target consumers directly. The *Cara* magazine was among the most successful methods as visitors often kept the advertisement and then wrote to the producer with orders when they returned home. A website was also developed, through which consumers and trade customers could place orders.

This respondent was very cognizant of portraying an upmarket, culturally conscious image in his use of imagery in product design and promotion; 'I don't want to be associated with shamrocks and shillelaghs'. A combination of choice of imagery in promotional materials, the logo of the business and the use of particular motifs in product design achieved the desired effect. Many of the images used by this respondent have already been discussed as examples in other chapters, so will only be referred to here.

Some product items had traditional Irish themes such as shamrocks, Celtic crosses and Celtic spirals, but a wide range of other more culturally and place specific images were also used in product design. A range of items borrowed from Irish legends relating to Oisín and Setanta. The Fiana and Fionn mac Cumhaill have strong Munster associations, one of the most famous of which relates to Fionn's grandson, Oisín. The Fiana were hunting in Killarney when Niamh of the golden hair persuaded Oisín to return with her to her otherworld kingdom. They galloped out to sea at Rossbeigh. After 300 years Oisín returned to search for his comrades. He climbed Ballaghisheen (Bealach Oisín) and then travelled to Glenasmole near Dublin where he was dismounted from his horse and turned into an old man. Legend has it that here he met St. Patrick and told him the stories of the Fiana (Barrington, 1976). This is how these stories are said to have come to be preserved in writing. The story of Setanta belongs to the Ulster Cycle of early Irish literature (Dillon, 1994). Setanta was the son of the god, Lug of the Long Arm of the Tuatha Dé Dannann, and Dechtire, sister of Conor mac Nessa, the King of Ulster. Because of a misunderstanding, he killed a hound which Culann, a friend of Conor mac Nessa, used to guard his lands. Setanta took over the guardianship role until a new hound could be trained, thus earning him the title Cúchulainn, Hound of Culann (Heaney, 1994).

Other collections were inspired by local archaeological features such as: the Riasc Cross, one of several early monuments dating from the 6th century at an ancient enclosure near Ballyferriter, on the Dingle Peninsula; the Sundial, located in the historic site of Kilmalkedar on the Dingle Peninsula and dating from the early Christian Phase (400-600 AD); the Kilshannig standing stone, a cross slab, again located on the Dingle Peninsula and dating from the seventh century; and, the Ogham Stone Collection, stones bearing an ancient linear script, the first known written language of Ireland, found in Kerry (Toal, 1995). In promotional materials, descriptions were given of all of these legends and features.

The logo of the business comprised the initials of the craftworker in a Celtic script, connoting Celticity and its associations (this will be discussed in more detail in Chapter 7). A wide range of promotional materials was used, including brochures, carrier bags, posters, display stands, catalogues and a website, all reinforcing similar themes. These included the craftsperson at work, incorporating the motifs of the producer engrossed in his work and the craftworker's tools in disarray (see above); the use of the landscape of the Kerry coastline, with a photograph of the craft product superimposed on it (similar to Figure 4.2); the craft product displayed on natural stone framed by foliage, thus located within nature (as discussed in Chapter 4); photographs of landscape scenes, equating the beauty of the region with the beauty of the product (Figure 4.4); written text comparing natural creation processes with the production of the craftworker ('An epic landscape has been a million years in the making – sculpted by ice and rain and quake … The craftsman too takes raw elements and shapes and hones and embellishes', 'From a land forged by nature's artistry comes a [product] collection with a timeless beauty'); the notion of the landscape as inspiration in written text ('The rhythms and images of Ireland's wild nature are the raw materials of her art – and are echoed in the quick and sensuous whorls and tracery of the [craftworker's] creations'); references to authentic craftsmanship in written text ('It is here that [producer's name] crafts his [product] according to the age-old traditions of the Celt'); and, the use of the Irish language, without an English translation, thus signifying "Irishness".

Several reasons were posited by the respondent for deciding to use these types of images, including: a personal love of the Irish language, a desire 'to give people a little impression of what Irish culture is about', to link in with the culture of the region to achieve higher prices and product differentiation, and to utilize every available method and advantage of the region in terms of the beauty of the landscape and the wealth of local archaeological features to promote his product. These types of motifs have become quite common in crafts production, particularly in this region. This is largely due to the success of this respondent who pioneered this type of imagery, particularly in export markets. Whatever the reasons for the use of place imagery, this strategy has positioned the product as the quintessence of authentic Irish/Celtic culture and tradition in this particular craft category.

In relation to other themes identified in academic writing, the 'holiday activities' imagery identified by Kneafsey (1997) were portrayed in the three regions. The most frequently mentioned pursuits were golf, horse riding, fishing and, in the Southwest, watersports. Traditional music was not referenced as often as sporting activities, although it was mentioned at least once in each region. Images of people/history/legend were found in all regions in both tourism and crafts literature; in crafts mainly in relation to these as a source of inspiration in product design (e.g. the legend of Oisín and Tír na nÓg, descriptions of the Claddagh ring[3] and the Derry na Flan chalice[4]). There were very few examples of vernacular architecture in any of the materials, the thatched cottage (Figure 5.1) being a notable exception, but images of spectacular architecture such as castles and period houses were very much in evidence.

Most of the tourist images discussed here are in sharp contrast to the images portrayed by Ireland's industrial and economic development organizations of a young, dynamic, modern country with a well-educated workforce and an advanced telecommunications and electronics industry. However, a new "Brand Ireland" tourism image, developed in 1995 by Bord Fáilte and the Northern Ireland Tourist Board, is designed to counteract the traditional image to some extent. It aims to close the perception gap that has opened up in many markets as regards Ireland's perceived image and the reality (Bord Fáilte, 1996a). Ireland is promoted as providing an emotive experience and offering opportunities for a wide range of recreational activities (Logue, 1996). The campaign concentrates on the strengths of the country in terms of its people, its warm welcome, its uniqueness as regards its green environment and the range of activities which can be enjoyed by visitors, regardless of age or interests (Bord Fáilte, 1996a). Bord Fáilte (1996b) acknowledged the impact of modern Irish culture on Ireland's image abroad, recognizing that 'success in music, literature, theatre, film and dance enhance Ireland's current international fashionability' (Bord Fáilte, 1996b in Prentice and Andersen, 2000, p. 499). This fashionability was incorporated into the "Brand Ireland" campaign which was preceded by two years of research 'designed to derive a brand positioning which would clearly reflect what Ireland as a holiday destination has to offer and which would also strongly appeal to the discerning visitor' (Bord Fáilte, 1996c in Prentice and Andersen, 2000, p. 499).

This attempt at brand repositioning reflects changing consumer demands and a changing market profile whereby European tourists with an interest in the environment and activity holidays are becoming more important, and the "roots" tourism of the U.S. and Britain which relied on the Tír na nÓg imagery of the country is becoming less so. In spite of this, more recent analyses of Irish tourism promotion abroad have found that the same actual images continue to be reproduced, with emphasis placed on idealized notions of rurality and nature, open spaces, romanticized work and timelessness (Markwick, 2001), and Ireland as the last remaining outpost of true authenticity (Graham, 2001).

The images used in the new Brand Ireland campaign found a stronger resonance in those identified in the promotional materials in the current sample than some of the more traditional images discussed. Numerous examples of most of these images (people, warm welcome, green environment, recreational activities) have already been identified and discussed. However, Ireland as an emotive experience was also evident in the promotional materials of several of both the tourism and crafts respondents. For example, the two tourism businesses highlighted in the previous chapter, Case Studies A and B, both used imagery in similar ways, employing a recognized aspect of the place image of County Sligo in order to create a distinct atmosphere for their products, one of a fantastic land steeped in heritage and mythology. Having established the mood of the place, an implicit invitation was extended to readers to 'indulg[e] in the wonders of this land of hearts (*sic*) desire'. In a similar manner, the crafts business discussed above, Case Study C, used the Irish language and legends, regional landscapes and local historical and archaeological features, in product design and promotion, with the intention of positioning the product as the quintessence of Irish culture in order to target a mainly tourist and foreign market. Implicit in the promotional message is an invitation to experience this unique Irish culture through consumption of these products.

Another crafts business (Business D), this time in the Midlands, utilized natural raw materials in its production and also incorporated elements of "Irishness", "naturalness", "landscape" and "Celticity" in the brand image. The use of poetry, the Irish language and textual references emphasizing the age of the materials and the artistry and craftsmanship of the producers in utilizing them invited consumers to experience a part of this Irish heritage through the consumption of the product, and combined to establish the product as the embodiment of Irishness and the Irish landscape, and as a unique piece of Irish Art.

The establishment of Business D was supported by a semi-state agency seven years prior to the interview, as a means of providing employment and utilizing local raw materials and crafts skills. Five years after establishment, the business became a co-operative wholly owned by the employees (five full-time and one part-time), who included a marketing manager. Financial and technical support was also received from FÁS and Enterprise Ireland. The craft products produced by this business were highly individual and specially commissioned sculptures and gift items and, from the outset, the corporate gift market was targeted. The owners wished to create a co-ordinated brand image which would be carried through the business name, logo, packaging, promotional materials and publicity. As an indication of the perceived importance of developing this image, they spent a similar sum on the initial promotion and marketing of the product as on constructing and equipping the workshop.

In choosing an image, the marketing manager looked to the product itself. The uniqueness of the product derived from the raw materials used; natural materials drawn from a particular Irish, especially Midlands (peat bog), landscape. It was decided to combine the elements of "Irishness", "naturalness" and "landscape" in the image; 'we wanted to show the rich Irish heritage and the unique atmosphere of the [particular landscape].' This was achieved in a variety of ways. Firstly, the business name combined an image of Irishness with an aspect of the raw material used. The logo of the business comprised the initials of the business name in Celtic lettering, connoting Irishness and images associated with Celticity, such as paganism, music, bards, Druids and craftsmanship.

A range of promotional materials was produced, including brochures, catalogues, headed note-paper, swing tags and a website. As well as photographs of the products, most of the literature contained a generic photograph of the environment from which the raw materials were drawn and included a descriptive piece of text discussing the formation of the landscape and the development of the materials over time. Emphasis was placed on the age of the materials and on the artistry and craftsmanship of the producers in utilizing them: '[the material] has lain hidden for over 5,000 years', 'The elegant and dramatic forms created by the young artists at the studio are a celebration of both our rich Irish heritage and the unique landscape and atmosphere of our [landscape]'. A poem which reflected the age and composition of the raw materials was used in most of the literature, in both English and Irish, *míle blíaín ag fás – a thousand years a growing*. This functioned as both an invocation of Irishness and as a way of connecting with the past, a theme which conveyed a long tradition of craftwork and authenticity.

In addition to using natural, local raw materials, some of the sculpted forms denoted Irish images, especially native birds, fish and plants. In catalogues and brochures, textual descriptions of the subject of the work were usually combined with photographs of the products; 'The corncrake is more often heard than seen ... the Shannon Callows near the [business] studio are one of the few remaining areas where corncrakes flourish'. As a further layer in the brand imaging process, only natural or recycled materials were used in the packaging of the products (paper, filling) and each item was individually presented in a handmade wooden box, created in the studio.

Having established an identity in the corporate market (through mail shots of promotional materials and one-to-one contact), free publicity was cultivated and utilized effectively to develop the product image in the public domain. To help establish the product as the embodiment of Irishness and the Irish landscape and as unique pieces of Irish Art, sculptures created by the business were offered to the Taoiseach of the day, members of the Irish government and other institutions, for presentation to visiting heads of state and other dignitaries. As a result of this exposure, retailers approached the business at the annual *Showcase Ireland* trade fair with requests to stock their products. To maintain the exclusive, quality image that had been developed and the perceived value attached to the product, the business chose only to deal with quality retail outlets which catered for the expensive end of the market. However, in an effort not to become dependent on the retail trade, as these outlets pay the lowest possible prices for the product, 80 percent of the business continued to come from the corporate market and commissioned work. The company also developed a website, which functioned as a promotional and marketing device through which consumers could place orders, in a further attempt to bypass the intermediary and thus garner the highest possible value from the sale. At the time of interview, the business had recently opened a showroom and retail outlet in the region which would be another source of direct sales.

Linked in with the pool of Irish images considered above (the clean, unspoilt environment) is the importance of Ireland's green image. Ireland as a country with a high quality environment is invoked increasingly in the marketing of food products and of tourism. In Britain, the United States and Europe, the colour green is acknowledged as an integral part of our national identity. It is fortunate that internationally this is the colour associated with environmental consciousness (Cotter, 1992; Drummery, 1992; Fahey, 1992). There were numerous examples in the promotional materials which attempted to tap into this green image. One such example from the tourism sector is a logo used by a cabin cruising company in the Midlands which consisted of a sketch of an anchor with a green shamrock inlaid (Figure 6.5).

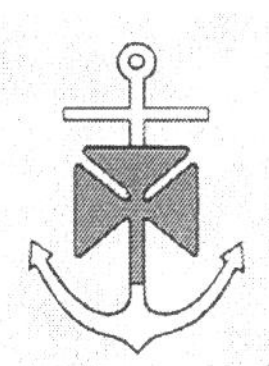

Figure 6.5 Anchor logo

The anchor is an index for the product itself, i.e. a boat, while the shamrock is a well known symbol for Ireland; thus the logo fell into the "product characteristics" category as well as "connection to place/use of regional imagery". The shamrock symbol also connotes other meanings. For example, it is utilized as the quality approval symbol of the Irish Tourist Board (Bord Fáilte), so its use here connotes quality. This association was reinforced on the company's brochure which displayed the Bord Fáilte shamrock symbol beside the word 'Ireland', both in the same shade of green that was used in the logo (Figure 6.6). As well as being associated with Ireland, the green also taps into the symbolism of environmental soundness.

Figure 6.6 Bord Fáilte symbol

Through a semiotic reading of images such as these, it is possible to demythologize the signs which make up the promotional messages being communicated to readers of these marketing materials. Such a reading allows us to examine the ways in which existing imagery of places are adapted and utilized in these promotions, which in turn serve to further propagate these often stereotypical images.

Notes

1 *The Playboy of the Western World*, John Millington Synge's comic depiction of rural western Ireland, caused a sensation when it was first produced in Dublin in 1907. Now considered a masterpiece, the play so offended Irish nationalists that riots broke out in the theatre because of its honest portrayal of local people.

2 The direct translation of Tír na nÓg is "land of eternal youth". It refers to a mystical land in Gaelic mythology whose inhabitants never grow old. The favorite legend of Tír na nÓg is that of the love between Niamh and Oisín, a goddess and a Celtic warrior.

3 A type of ring dating back some 400 years and associated with the Claddagh fishing village overlooking Galway Bay.

4 A fine example of early-medieval Irish metalwork, the Derrynaflan Chalice dates from 800 AD and was discovered in 1980, in the environs of the ancient monastic settlement of Derrynaflan, an island in Littleton Bog, County Tipperary.

Chapter 7

The Role of Place in the Production of 'Uniqueness'

Place imagery has a role in producing "uniqueness", and images which symbolize regional distinctiveness can be used as a method of product differentiation, especially when this distinctiveness is equated with quality and authenticity. Bell and Valentine (1997) consider the social and cultural meanings of food consumption and examine the role of food in creating identity at a range of different spatial levels, from the body, to the home, community, city, region, nation and globe. They define the region as 'a product of both human and physical processes: a natural landscape and a peopled landscape ... a powerful way of thinking of place and identity' and argue that 'the physical and human landscapes are seen as together producing ... uniqueness' (Bell and Valentine, 1997, p. 153). The example of bottled water is used to illustrate how this uniqueness can also equate to quality. This is a product which is often identified with a particular place, which can be traced back to an exact source, and this brings with it impressions of purity and naturalness.

Quality is identified as a method of creating a segment in the market. Successful product differentiation which provides consumer confidence, on which customer loyalty is based, may be able to command a premium price. There is no one agreed definition of quality, but it is recognized that it has a number of different dimensions. Its operational dimension involves 'ensuring conformance and, more importantly, fitness for purpose or the extent to which the product or service consistently meets the customer's needs' (O'Neill and Black, 1996, p. 16). As well as ensuring consistency of products and services, as an objective concept, quality is associated with compliance with recognized and independently adjudicated standards (Excellence Ireland, 1997). Complex systems of control are also in place in many areas of activity to measure and assure standards of "total quality", based on objective measurable criteria throughout the production process (Dawson, 1994). However, quality also has a more subjective dimension which relates to the customer's perceptions of the product or service, in other words, quality is defined by the customer based on his/her expectations rather than on a set of objective criteria. These subjective definitions of quality which reflect particularistic expressions of tastes and styles vary between places, time periods and social groups (Bell and Valentine, 1997). Quality features are also based on various criteria relating to very specific characteristics of materials, ingredients, methods of production, presentation, the character that attaches to the place of delivery and the socio-cultural context within which the product is purchased

(Ilbery and Kneafsey, 2000). These features are particularly relevant in relation to niche food, rural tourism services and quality crafts (Cowan and Sexton, 1997; Cawley *et al.*, 1999). Increasingly consumer perception of product or service quality is being used as a competitive tool and is an important factor in determining long term business profitability (Parker, 1990/91; Quinn, M. 1994). Quality can, therefore, be described as 'a "positional" characteristic, something which is above minimum standards and which gives a product or service (or process, company or region) a cutting edge over its rivals' (Ilbery *et al.*, 1999, p. 3).

Another example of uniqueness equating with quality is the *appellation d'origine* which is used to symbolise regional distinctiveness (Barham, 2003). This assures the customer that 'thanks to the combination of environmental conditions and carefully regulated "craft" production processes, they know precisely what they are eating or drinking' (Bell and Valentine, 1997, p. 155). Because of the fears over food safety, there is a greater demand for products from an identifiable geographical source (Morris, 2000). This provides marketing opportunities for local rural economies to link their products to the region's landscapes and culture through the use of regional imagery. Locally produced products can 'contribute to place distinctiveness in terms of specific place-related characteristics such as style, ingredients and production methods' (Ilbery and Kneafsey, 1998, p. 334). In relation to rural development and diversification of the rural economy, ways of gaining competitive advantage are particularly relevant in order to compensate for a generally small scale of production. This was recognized by the Rural Development Policy Advisory Group (Government of Ireland, 1997) when it recommended that

> every effort should be made to encourage the production of high quality raw materials and to ensure that maximum value added linked to market opportunities is secured in the processing of these raw materials in the rural areas concerned (p. 54).

This reflects a recent OECD (1995) report which suggests that 'niche markets and the activities to satisfy those markets have positive implications for rural development' (p. 14). Niche products are those which use product differentiation and market segmentation to distinguish them from mass produced products. In relation to rural products, Guerry (1995) has identified two types of differentiation:

> a) Special brands or quality, or limited quantities such as:
> - territorial brands, quality labels or certificates of origin;
> - high quality linked to traditional methods, raw materials and know-how used to make local products;
> - limited quantity, stemming from the size of production capacity of the area.
>
> b) Extreme specialization in terms of supply with the specialization applying to the product, marketing, promotion, etc. (p. 69).

In other words, differentiation can be based on area specificity or territoriality, as well as some original feature of the product itself. In the promotion of rural niche products, the use of specific landscapes, cultural traditions or historic monuments in promotion can create territorial linkages which can function as a niche marketing strategy. The EU has also expressed strong support for the promotion of quality products and services where quality is defined as being associated with particular rural areas or origins. The *Opinion of the Committee of the Regions of September 1996* (Commission of the European Communities, 1996) refers to the importance of quality guarantees and the certification of enterprises and products in general. It points out that attested regional origin of a product, as a guarantee of quality, is of increasing importance 'at a time when trust between producers and consumers is more difficult to establish on larger markets' (p. 2). Legislation to protect geographical origin and special character, in the case of agricultural products and foodstuffs, has been introduced by the EU: Regulation 2081/92/EEC protects geographical indications and designations of origin (*appellations d'origine*), Regulation 2082/92/EEC provides for the award of certificates of specific character, and Regulation 2092/91/EEC makes provision for the labelling and advertising of the products of biological agriculture. In comparison to other European countries, very few Irish regional products had been registered under EEC Regulations 2081/92 or 2082/92. This absence of registration highlights a poorly developed appreciation of the potential marketing strengths provided by associations between particular food products and their region of production, in Ireland.

Much academic enquiry to date pertaining to connection to place as a niche marketing approach has focused on food products and much of this has centred around the concepts of typicality and embeddedness. Typicality, or the idea of cuisine de terroir, sees food production and consumption as being

> grounded in the landscape – soil, climate, growers and suppliers that have been historically assembled and nurtured into a complementary and evolutionary network keenly tuned to local growing conditions, markets and each other's needs (O'Neill and Whatmore, 2000, p. 133).

The quality of typical food products resides in a 'cultural appreciation' of the uniqueness of the localized components which make up the product (Miele and Murdoch, 2002, p. 324). It is not difficult to imagine how this same 'cultural appreciation' can be applied to other locally produced products and services, particularly in light of Winter's (2003) findings in relation to embeddedness and the new food economy. In a study of food purchases in rural localities in England and Wales, it was found that patterns of food purchasing revealed a defensive politics of localism rather than a strong turn to quality based food production. This turn to the local may have implications for other rural products such as crafts and tourism services. Therefore, it is not only food products which can benefit from linking with the region. As Bell and Valentine (1997) have noted, 'almost any product which has some tie to place – no matter how "invented" this may be – can be sold as embodying that place' (p. 155). Crafts products can construct regional associations either through a direct link (e.g. use of local raw materials/craftspersonship) or through an "invented" link (e.g. using a regional brand name). This is of particular benefit to those craftspeople who sell their product to tourists as 'crafts or other souvenirs can serve as tangible evidence of having found the authentic or having participated in the indigenous life of a community' (Littrell, 1990, p. 199). Also, several Gaeltacht areas have participated in a pilot project to develop a tourism ECO-label under the EU LIFE programme which sought to protect unique characteristics which can be used for marketing. The LIFE programme stemmed from the Fifth Environmental Action Programme of the EU and proposed 'to achieve a balance between human activity, economic development and environmental protection by an impartial, yet clearly defined, sharing of responsibility' (Ó Cinnéide, 1999, p. 102). These examples also relate to the 'commodification of the region' by emphasizing the region's selling points (Bell and Valentine, 1997, p. 161).

In order to maximize the economic benefits of tourism, linkages between tourism and other sectors in the region, e.g. food and crafts, are seen as advantageous (Telfer and Wall, 1996). It has been argued that tourists search for authenticity (MacCannell, 1973; 1976). Authenticity has become a major selling point in the promotion of tourist destinations; 'Perhaps the most common motif in travel columns is the hotel, restaurant or sight "just off the beaten track" ' (Culler, 1988, p. 158). In particular, in recent years, tourists increasingly search for traditional social values and links with the past (MacCannell, 1976; Urry, 1990; MacCannell, 1992; Nuryanti, 1996; McIntosh and Prentice, 1999; Wang, 1999). This has manifested itself in the rise of alternative forms of rural, cultural and heritage tourism as already discussed. Consuming locally produced crafts products, including food, contributes to the authenticity of the tourism experience (Littrell, 1990; Littrell *et al.*, 1993; Bessière, 1998).

From an examination of the promotional materials of the sampled crafts and tourism producers, as well as interview responses, it would appear that they agree with Bell and Valentine's (1997) assessment that landscapes can contribute to the production of uniqueness in such products. In the Southwest in particular, but represented in all regions, location was identified by respondents as a distinguishing feature of their product, as well as an important factor in ensuring overall quality. Most craftworkers described the uniqueness of their product in terms of the originality of design, colour and finish, as well as 'quality' *per se*, raw materials and aspects of production technique. However, for many of these producers design and colour were commonly inspired by local landscapes, and local raw materials were frequently used in production. These features were emphasized in promotion to establish the unique nature of the product. In the Southwest, using local imagery was explicitly mentioned as being important as a distinguishing feature.

For accommodation providers, using quality food was important in terms of producing a quality product and in distinguishing their business from others. Use of local produce was particularly highlighted in the Northwest and Southwest. A reason for this may be that the former region has an emerging reputation for organic food produce, whilst the latter is recognized for its artisanal food production. The actual house was also seen as a distinctive feature for accommodation providers, particularly in the case of historic houses with established links to the region. Ambience, in terms of peace and quiet, hospitality and 'homeliness', was emphasized in the Midlands and Northwest, whilst in the Southwest, location was mentioned explicitly as a distinguishing factor. A number of respondents in the Midlands also referred to location, meaning their specific setting on a river, an esker, near woodlands, and so on, rather than their regional location.

For many crafts producers, showing photographs of recognizable places was part of this process of equating the product with the place and imbuing it with place characteristics, thus making it unique to that place. I have discussed this in detail in Chapter 4 in relation to Figures 4.1, 4.2, 4.3 and 4.4. The use of the Irish language in promotion was another part of this process, this time imbuing the product with unique characteristics of "Irishness". An example of this in the Midlands, '*míle blíaín ag fás – a thousand years a growing*' implied a connection with the past, as well as with the place, while in the Southwest, '*Bréagtar bean le seod súirí*' was more ambiguous. In the first instance, the connection to Ireland and Irish culture was not the only message being conveyed (i.e. the connection with the past was also an important connotation), thus an English translation was included in the slogan. The second motto, however, is unquestionably an invocation of "Irishness" and the literal meaning is almost entirely unimportant as the vast majority of the readers will have very little or no knowledge of the Irish language. For the slogan to work, readers need only recognize it as being Irish.

Slogans 'implant images in the minds of readers' (Barke and Harrop, 1994, p. 99) and are a useful ways of doing so (Burgess, 1982). An interesting fact is that more than 60 percent of the slogans present in the sample occurred in the promotional literature of respondents in the Midlands. As speculated in Chapter 3, one possible reason for this proliferation of slogans was that an image of this region had not yet become established in the minds of consumers, therefore, more producers used slogans to convey a variety of different images in the hope that some would become familiar. The fact that the largest proportion of the slogans used in the Midlands fell into the "connection to place/use of regional imagery" category supports this speculation. Consumers were encouraged to buy crafts '*from the heart of Ireland*', to come and enjoy the '*Midland magic*' because '*It's Central, It's Special*'. In the other regions, producers were more likely to use slogans which implanted positive images of their own product in the minds of readers ("product characteristics/praise") than images of the region. Readers were told that the products offered '*A full day's entertainment*' and '*A great afternoon out for all the family*' or were '*enchanted creation*[s]' displaying '*gracious elegance*'. Of course, slogans extolling the virtues of respondents' products were also used in the Midlands, such as '*splendid food in a glorious setting*' and '*the supreme gift*'.

In the Northwest and Southwest, the "connection to place" slogans rarely referred to the region specifically, or to an area or feature within the region. Rather, products were '*Part of Ireland's best kept secret*', '*Ireland's finest castle of its period*' or '*Ireland's most exciting* [product]'. The significance of slogans such as these is two-fold: the product is most definitely Irish, therefore embodies all of the qualities and myths of "Irishness" that exist; and, the product is positively differentiated from all others of its type in the country. Only two respondents used a slogan which referred to a specific place within the regions and both used the same one: '*Country House Comfort in Carrick-on-Shannon/Kenmare*'. This is a very explicit example of Gold's (1994) argument that, because the meaning of promotional messages are created and negotiated within the wider ideological context, this habitually leads to conformity. Promotional literature becomes increasingly homogenous as the same types of imagery and language are used time after time, because producers and consumers of images share comparable ideological perspectives. The ideology operating here is that of the rural idyll, '*Country House Comfort*', but in an urban setting and with all of the conveniences that suggests.

Written text in promotional materials made more explicit the connection to place which gave the craft its uniqueness. The location of production was often described (e.g. 'the unique landscape and atmosphere of our bogland', 'we are located in the beautiful setting of...', '... where the natural beauty around her home inspires her designs', 'Inspired by the soft tones and greenness of Ireland'), implying that the product would not be the same were it made anywhere else. Other textual images of place related to the use of local/Irish raw materials (see Chapter 5 for further examples).

In relation to crafts, the fact that the product was handmade added to its uniqueness, individuality and integrity ('I like to work ... by hand because it creates the opportunity to develop a special relationship with the material and the subject matter'). As Bell and Valentine (1997) point out it is 'the physical and human landscapes ... together' (p. 153) which produce the uniqueness. The craftsmanship of the producers, who were often explicitly described as being Irish or from a particular county, and the long tradition of the craft, sometimes handed down from father to son and from Master Craftsman to apprentice, were two motifs which added to the uniqueness of the product. Use of local or Irish raw materials was the third factor of significance in terms of Bell and Valentines' (1997) argument. By using place specific materials, the product was infused with part of that place, making it unique to the area ('The timber ... is approximately 300 years old and came from an old estate in [name of town]'). The notion of landscape as inspiration was also part of this process. As discussed above, the product would be a very different one if it were produced anywhere else.

Some of the logos analyzed in the crafts sector related to more than one theme when the sign consisted of more than one element. One logo which fell into more than one category and exemplifies many of the elements discussed above was that used by a craftsperson in the Northwest who restores antique stained glass windows and designs and manufactures new windows. She used a sample of a stained glass design which itself was adapted from the Book of Kells as her logo, surrounded by the words, '*Restoration*', '*Creation*' and '*Inspiration*' in a medieval style typeface (Figure 7.1). This sign can be read in a number of different ways and falls into three different categories ("product characteristics"; "connecting with the past"; "connection to place/use of regional imagery"). At a denotative level, the image and the text represent the type of work she does, i.e. restores and creates stained glass windows. The word 'inspiration' connotes artistic talent, imagination and design, as well as implying that the work itself is inspiring to the viewer. The Book of Kells image also connotes artistry, the use of bright colours and represents a work that is long-lasting, has endured from a past era (also reflected in the medieval style lettering) and is world renowned as an example of artistic endeavour. In addition, a latent religious symbolism is present in the sign, echoed in the use of the word 'creation' which has divine associations. The selection of such a symbolic image was quite deliberate as many of this craftworker's consumers were religious institutions. The Book of Kells is also a recognizably Irish image and inspires many craftspeople in product design.

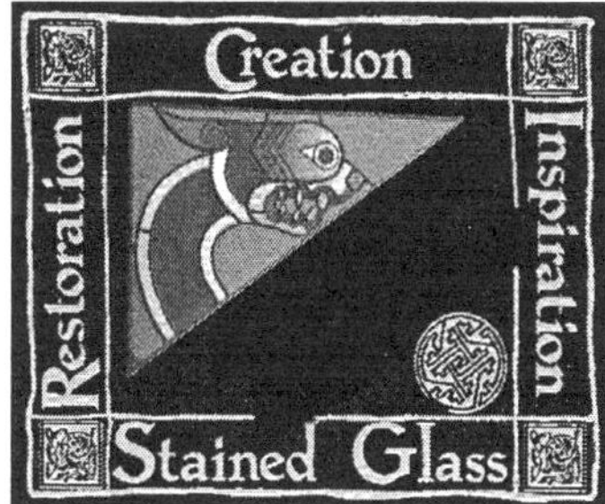

Figure 7.1 Stained glass logo (business name removed)

Simpler logos, while containing less elements within the sign, can also provide varied readings. For example, two craftworkers, one each in the Midlands and Southwest, used their business name initials only (one was the craftworker's own name) in a Celtic lettering typeface as their business logos. In both cases the letters are linked together (Figures 7.2 and 7.3).

Figure 7.2 Celtic lettering logo 1

Figure 7.3 Celtic lettering logo 2

At first glance, these symbols simply denote the name of the company or craftworker, which was usually printed underneath the logo. However, both of these businesses produced products which had strong links with their place of production, either through using natural, local raw materials or through the use of Celtic symbols and archaeological relics in product design. The use of the Celtic typeface connotes this Irish connection, as well as evoking the products themselves. Apart from being a war-like people, the Celts are associated with a host of different images including paganism, music, bards, Druids and craftsmanship, in particular a tradition of metalwork and jewellery (Chapman, 1992; Delaney, 1993). As in the case of the business discussed in the previous chapter, the symbolic use of the Celtic lettering also suggests these latent meanings.

In relation to tourism services, several different methods were used to infuse the product with the distinctive characteristics of the region. Heritage attraction products, for example, embodied part of the history of the particular place and could not be located elsewhere. The particular unique terrain of the landscape gave golf courses their distinctive features, whether that be links, hilly terrain or located beside a unique/well-known place. The following case studies illustrate these two types of tourism enterprises which were surveyed in the three regions: heritage attractions and golf courses. Both of these types of products have strong place connections which were utilized extensively in promotion. The former heritage attractions comprised sites of local, regional or national cultural, ecclesiastical, environmental, industrial, natural or scientific interest. The latter product was etched out of the landscape itself, so the place was the product. In any promotion, product images are used but in these cases, the products were also part of the imagery of the place.

Business E was a heritage attraction which *per se* was mentioned by producers and organizations as an image of the Midlands. The product had strong connections to the region and the history of the product and the owners was interwoven with the history of the area, so the product itself (a 17th century castle and gardens) was the regional image used to promote it. The property bore the name of the local town. The house was privately owned by the family who had lived there for generations, but the grounds and out-buildings had been leased on a long-term basis to a charity foundation which had been established to preserve and develop the attraction. Members of the family continued to be closely involved in the management and promotion of the property.

The product comprised a number of different features of historical, scientific and environmental interest. One of the features (formal gardens) had been available for viewing for 35 years prior to the interview and, with the establishment of the foundation in the 1980s, the other features were developed for public consumption. As a charity foundation and a heritage site, the product was entitled to a variety of European and Irish government supports for restoration and development, and received corporate sponsorship. In addition to employing six staff on a full-time basis and two more part-time, the business was entitled to subsidized labour through FÁS training and Community Employment schemes.

No promotion of the product was conducted when it was first opened to the public, the market was mainly a local one and the owners just ‘opened the doors and people trickled in’. Visitors also came from particular international special interest groups, among whom the property and its features were already well-known. After developing the other features, a marketing campaign was put in place which combined brochure and booklet distribution, mail shots to special interest groups, membership of national and regional marketing groups, targeting tour operators and creating a website. The textual and photographic images used in the promotional literature were primarily of the product itself, the owners and their respective histories within the area, as well as the history of the development of the product as a public attraction. Some of the literature also contained limited factual information about the local town, its location in Ireland, and the availability of tourist facilities. Regional imagery *per se* was not seen as important by the respondent, in fact the location was seen as a disadvantage. It was recognized, however, that 'it wouldn't be the same product anywhere else'. Like many other heritage attractions of its kind in the three regions, whilst the image used in promotion was of the product and no conscious effort was made to use regional images, the fact that the product itself was a regional attraction meant that place imagery was inevitably used.

Business F was similar to Business D in that the product was the regional image used in promotion or, more accurately in this case, the place was the product. This business was a family owned golf club, which had been established three years prior to the interview as a means of exploiting under-utilized farmland. The land was located on undulating terrain, which made it difficult for farming, but ideal as a golf course. The sandy composition of the hills also provided very good drainage, which meant that the course was playable during the winter. Capital assistance was received from the County Enterprise Board for the initial development of the course and Christy O'Connor Jnr., an Irish golfer of international repute, was employed as designer. The business employed six people on a full-time basis and four seasonal staff, excluding the owners.

A multi-faceted promotional campaign was put in place to launch the product, including brochure distribution, television advertising, direct approaches to tour operators and exploiting the reputation of Christy O'Connor Jnr. to generate publicity among golf writers and publications. From the beginning, the unique selling points of the business were identified as being the uniqueness of the terrain and the reputation of the course designer, so these were the elements emphasized in all promotional materials. The course was named after the hills on which it was located and photographs and descriptions of the topography were included in the literature; 'Nature has sculpted the landscape into a series of valleys and plateaux ... which together with the existence of natural lakes and woodlands makes it ideal golfing terrain'. Reference was also made to the geological formation of the landscape over time. The local town was discussed, in terms of its central location, accommodation and facilities. Such place imagery was used in conjunction with photographs of, and quotes from, Christy O'Connor Jnr.; 'Designing [name of product] gave me enormous satisfaction ... [it] is the only links type course I know of, which makes winter golf a pleasure'.

Over time the business collaborated with other golf courses and hotels in the region in a joint promotional campaign, *Golf in the Heart of Ireland*. A brochure was produced and distributed to tour operators, travel agents and tourist offices. This too made use of place imagery in different forms. A slogan invited readers to '*Sample the magic of the Midlands*' and the text discussed the location of the region, local attractions, activities and accommodation, all 'in a beautiful rural setting'.

These enterprises represent two types of tourism products surveyed in each of the study regions: heritage attractions and golf courses. Both of these categories of products exhibited strong linkages to place which were used extensively in promotion. Images of the product are used in most tourism promotion, but in these cases, the products also happened to be part of the imagery of the place: heritage attractions through their historical or cultural connection to the location; and golf courses because they are etched out of the landscape itself, so the place is the product.

In relation to accommodation products, photographs and descriptions of regional landscapes and landscape features described a unique holiday experience which could be experienced by staying in that particular place. Historic houses, in particular, provided visitors with a distinctive experience – nowhere else could one achieve the same ambience. Slogans also declared the importance of location as endowing special characteristics on the product – '*It's Central, It's Special*', '*Midland Magic*'. Descriptions of the location of the business within the region 'nestling at the foot of the Slieve Bloom mountains' added to the uniqueness of the holiday experience. The largest proportions of textual images in the promotional literature of tourism respondents in the Midlands and Northwest related to the "connection to place/use of regional imagery" theme, followed by the "functional information about the product" category, whereas in the Southwest, the reverse obtained. In the Northwest and Southwest, the top two categories comprised circa 40 percent and 30 percent of the textual images, whilst in the Midlands, the top category comprised more than 50 percent of the images and the second less than 15 percent. As already discussed, businesses in the Midlands were attempting to create an image for the region where none was felt to exist, so one of the main objectives of their promotional literature was to inform readers of the various attractions in the region. Conversely, because the image of the Southwest was already so well developed, respondents did not need to place as much importance in their literature on persuading readers of the region's appeal. Instead, their main objective was to divert consumers away from their competitors within the region, thus the emphasis on providing practical information about the product itself. Businesses in the Northwest fell somewhere in between the two in terms of promoting the advantages of the region, because the region was felt to already have a certain image attached to it, but one which was not yet as well developed as that of the Southwest.

Within the "connection to place/use of regional imagery" category, the most frequently occurring theme in the three regions was listing or describing local or regional attractions and facilities. As discussed in Chapter 5, the same few images of the regions were used again and again (e.g. the River Shannon, the Slieve Bloom mountains and Clonmacnoise in the Midlands). The second most frequently occurring motif within this category in the three regions was descriptions of the location of the business within the region. Many of these references in the Midlands related to the product's centrality within Ireland: '... ideally situated in the heart of Ireland – nestling at the foot of the Slieve Bloom mountains'; 'All at the crossroads of Ireland'; 'in the very heart of Ireland'; 'in the very centre of Ireland'. In the Northwest and Southwest, these descriptions generally referred to the product's proximity to various regional attractions: 'situated beneath Knocknarea Mountain'; 'situated under the shadow of famed Benbulben'; 'situated 2km from Sligo town under historic Knocknarea mountain and overlooking Sligo Bay'; 'situated mid way between Killarney and Killorglin – just off the Ring of Kerry'; 'Idyllically set at the head of Bantry Bay'; . '... within strolling distance of the splendid harbour and yacht marina along with many historic sites, shops and the unique pubs and restaurants of Kinsale'. Again, the assumption is that readers would already have some positive perception of these locations and attractions, therefore the businesses' proximity to them is an advantage. On the other hand, in the Midlands, a lack of awareness of regional attractions (apart, perhaps, from the Slieve Bloom mountains and the River Shannon, which were mentioned), as well as a desire to exploit the perceived locational advantage of centrality, as discussed in relation to maps in Chapter 3, were the motives for using such images. Description of the location of the business in terms of its proximity to major cities and airports was another recurrent motif in this region, much more so than in the Northwest and Southwest, which also supports this conjecture.

In the Midlands and Northwest, descriptions of the immediate location of the premises were also common: '... surrounded by mature trees, extensive gardens and 100 acres of farmland'; 'wake up to the beautiful scenery that surrounds this Country House'; 'in a picturesque parkland setting'; 'situated on 1 hectare (2.5 acres) with its own river frontage'. Such images generally described the beauty of the surrounding scenery, as well as pointing out its advantages in terms of various special interest activities (fishing, walking, gardening). These types of descriptions were not common in the Southwest, perhaps because it was not deemed necessary to wax lyrical about the advantages of the immediate location of the business as the surrounding region itself and its features were appealing enough to the reader.

As well as the physical landscapes, the human landscapes were important in adding to the individuality of tourism products. Personal service by owners, as described in text and photographs and the care and friendliness of staff contributed to the product (see Chapter 4 for a full description). Because of the locations in rural areas, visitors were offered tranquil, relaxing holidays away from the hectic modern world. As shown, the paradigmatic choice of such imagery adds to the uniqueness of these products and regions, differentiating them from other places (again, see Chapter 4). As well as tranquil, relaxing holidays, the largely urban-based visitors targeted by the promotional imagery were also offered a unique experience through explicit references to "rurality". Apart from "landscape/natural environment" images, motifs included agricultural references ('a sight not to be missed is the local farmer's cows ...', 'see at first hand the workings of a farm in rural Ireland'), contrasts to modern, urban living ('an ideal location away from town and city', 'traditional cottage in rural setting', 'largely untouched by the industrial revolution') and references to the rural countryside ('the magnificent countryside … is there to be explored', '… in a beautiful rural setting'). Such examples provide tangible evidence of the utilization of territorial/place linkages as a method of niche product marketing.

Chapter 8

The Role of Place Myths in Creating Social Spaces

In this chapter I consider the role of place myths in the creation of social spaces. Whilst case studies have been used as illustrative tools throughout the book, I make more extensive use of this device in this chapter to demonstrate a number of key points. Shields (1991) has argued that a 'discourse of space', which is composed of perceptions of places and regions, is fundamental to our everyday understandings of ourselves and our reality. Tourism images are part of this 'discourse of space' and it is increasingly recognized that tourism promotional bodies contribute greatly to the creation of the imagined geographies of places abroad through place representation. Waitt (1997), for example, warns that all national tourism promotion bodies have the authority to endorse landscapes that are part of the 'iconography of nationhood' (p. 57). O'Connor (1993) agrees that place representations influence cultural and national identities because 'the way in which we see ourselves is substantially determined by the way in which we are seen by others' (p. 68). Kneafsey (1995) has also argued that 'landscape is being interpreted in new ways for tourism... the interpretation of landscapes can contribute to constructions of place and identity, acting as a powerful symbolic and cultural icon' (p. 136). In her work, she examines how tourism influences the form of conceptions of rurality, tradition, authenticity and identity. Through exploring the ways in which a particular aspect of the landscape of North West Mayo is being developed as a tourist attraction she illustrates the hypothesis that, whilst place and identity are culturally constructed, dynamic concepts which are open to various interpretations, the commodification of tourist destinations involves a fixing of exclusivist meanings to places. These images projected in place promotion define the boundaries of experience. In other words, the 'images define what is beautiful, what should be experienced and with whom one should interact' (Dann, 1996, p. 79).

Lash and Urry (1994) see it as a characteristic of modernity, that social spaces develop which can be completely or somewhat reliant on the visitors to those places, and that those visitors are drawn by the place-myths that frame and comprise such places. Urry (1995) uses the Lake District in England as an example of a space which possesses a particular place-myth which developed when writers visited the region and wrote about the landscape in a particular picturesque style which is now known as English Romanticism. Another example of a space which possesses a particular place myth is the West of Ireland (Nash, 1993). The development of the myth of the West as embodying all that is truly Irish has been documented (Chapter 6) and, as discussed, it was clear that this myth was tapped into in the promotional materials analyzed. Places such as these remain fundamental to the geographical imagination and the place-myths do not change easily, even when the characteristics of the place change significantly (Shields, 1991). The reason for this is that 'changes necessitate not just an adjustment of the myth ... but a restructuring of the entire mythology and the development of new metaphors by which ideology is presented' (Shields, 1991, p. 256).

However, especially in relation to tourism, advantages have been identified in not challenging particular place myths. In discussing the semiotic production of tourist spaces, Hughes (1998) identifies that 'Like the Irish, the Scots have realized that there is money to be made from conforming to a stereotypical image, however bogus it may be' (p. 25). He goes on to highlight that, as well as tapping into place myths in promotion, tourism plays an active role 'in creating local geographies, semiotically, through the medium of place representation' (Hughes, 1998, p. 30). Johnson (2000) agrees that the significance of the images of place represented in tourism promotional materials

> does not reside solely in identifying whether they are effective or authentic expositions of place ... it is their role as part of a larger network of circulated ideas about the nature of place and the past which is of import (p. 260).

In other words, tourism has become a significant way of organizing meanings in space and this 'semiological differentiation of space has become a highly self-conscious ... process' (Hughes, 1998, p. 20). Depictions of places are intentionally constructed to appeal to the tourist market and therein lies the crux; place representation by tourism promoters is a deliberate form of 'spatialisation' (see Chapter 5). This study argues that crafts producers and other regional businesses which use links to place/regional imagery to market their products also contribute to this process through the evocation of, and contribution to, the particular place-myths. As increasing numbers of places scramble for limited consumers and more and more products use place imagery in promotion, the social spatialisation of places can no longer be said to evolve naturally, if it ever could.

As well as promoting their actual product, many tourism businesses also promoted their location through the use of very specific place imagery. Such use of imagery contributes to the deliberate social spatialisation of these places. Two examples from the Southwest illustrate the point. The first tourism business (Business G) used a wide range of promotional materials, primarily a variety of brochures targeted at different niche markets. Most of these materials used the same format and emphasized similar themes, to ensure a co-ordinated image. This product primarily centred around water-based activities and an important feature was its location. Because of this, promotional materials promoted the place as well as the product. Like Business F (discussed in the previous chapter), the second tourism example (Business H) chosen in this region was a relatively newly-established golf course which used a place name and regional imagery in its promotion. However, whereas in Business F it was a relatively unknown, hilly terrain which gave the product its distinctiveness and was used as the brand image, in this case it was a location beside a very well known town in the Southwest which was the unique selling point. The place name was again used as the product name and emphasis was placed on the 'setting with spectacular views of [well-known place]'.

Business G was established 17 years prior to the interview because the owners 'wanted to find a business that would finance a lifestyle of living here', so from the beginning, place image was of fundamental importance in the motivation for business establishment. The enterprise started as a one-person operation providing lessons in and facilities for one activity only and developed into a multi-activity centre with accommodation, employing 10 full-time, 15 part-time and 15 seasonal staff. The original marketing of the product involved local advertising and attendance at local consumer shows. At the time of interview, a wide range of methods was used, including brochure distribution, mail shots to consumers and travel agents, telesales, advertising in national and specialist publications, and circulating posters locally and regionally.

The product was named after its location, which was a deliberate attempt by the owners to 'sell the location as well as the product'. The enterprise was located on a bay in West Cork and most of the materials included a photograph of the product, as seen from a distance and incorporating the bay and the surrounding countryside. The logo of the business was made up of a sea-bird flying over rocks which rose out of a body of water. This was a depiction of actual rocks located in the inlet. Photographs of other views of the bay, often including people enjoying the activities of the business, were also common. Most of the brochures were aimed at particular niche markets and the photographs which contained people always reflected the target market, with the bay and scenery in the background. A more general brochure aimed at a wider market also contained a photograph and a textual description of a local town. Textual descriptions of the place, in terms of 'the beauty of the location', 'the spectacular views', and the repetition of the name of the area and the name of the centre were included in most materials. Other motifs evident in the literature of this business were photographs of the owners, a wealth of functional information particularly in niche brochures and recommendations from previous consumers ('Our trip to [product name] exceeded by far any other outing we have had').

Although the basic product was in existence as a member-owned, 9-hole golf course for 23 years prior to the interview, Business H did not become a fully developed tourist product until 22 years later when it launched an 18-hole championship course with a professional marketing manager and business office. Since then, 50 percent of its business came from tourists. Funds were obtained from a number of sources for the product development, including grants from LEADER and Bord Fáilte, fund-raising and borrowings from a golf society. This course was also designed by Christy O'Connor Jnr., and his photograph, signature and positive comments were used in promotion.

From the mid-1980s onwards, a marketing committee was established from among the members to identify the target market and compile a brochure and promotional package. Tour operators, other golf clubs and local accommodation premises were targeted by mail shots and the club became a member of regional and national marketing groups. They also secured citations in golfing guides, as well as advertisements and free publicity in local newspapers and specialist golf publications.

Two pieces of promotional literature from this business were contained in the sample. As identified, the major themes used were its location on the site of a well-known place in West Cork, a place recognized in song, folklore and historical tradition, and the endorsements of Christy O'Connor Jnr. Photographs of the course were used, but almost all of these included a view of the place in the background. Photographs of the place itself and the signpost leading to it were also included, in case there was any doubt about the location. As well as textual descriptions of the immediate area, 'an area renowned for its beauty', images of the wider West Cork region were used. These included: 'the area is renowned for its natural home-grown produce and excellent restaurants', the 'creamy pint of black stout', 'traditional music and craic', Bantry House and Gardens, Whiddy Island, the 1796 Armada Centre, Glengarriff's Garnish Island, the Beara Peninsula, the cliffs of Mizen, and Gougane Barra. In addition, the *Fuchsia* brand was used with accompanying text identifying the product as a member of West Cork Tourism.

The *Fuchsia* brand is a symbol of quality as well as being a regional brand (see Chapter 4). The quality of the product was reinforced in references to the course designer: a history of the development of the course mentioned his contribution, and a photograph of the famous golfer, as well as a large signed quotation, took prominent positions in the materials. Another quality recommendation was the reference to the international membership of the club, with 'over 100 [members] ... from all over Europe'. The respondent expressed an intention to convey an image of a cosmopolitan social club rather than a competitive golf club in promotional literature. This was reflected in the descriptions of ancillary services and activities available in the clubhouse and locally, and in the descriptions of local attractions and scenery. Other golf club brochures placed more emphasis on describing the particularities of the individual golf holes and on listing competitions and events that had been held.

These examples illustrate the ways in which some businesses seemed to promote their particular locations in a deliberate way as well as their products. In the first instance, this was due to the fact that the location was of primary importance in providing the holiday experience, i.e. water based activities. In the second instance, a positive image of the place already existed in the public consciousness, so by promoting the place with the product, an attempt was being made to equate the two in the minds of the reader.

Dilley (1986) argues that, whatever images may be portrayed by individual businesses such as those described, the significance of place promotional materials advocated by 'official' tourism bodies lies in the assertion that 'this is how the countries themselves wish to be seen' (p. 64). However, it is not only at the national level that tourism promotion bodies can advocate particular landscapes and, indeed, it is not only tourism organizations that use place images in promotion. I have identified a range of national, regional and local organizations which have become involved in place promotion to a greater or lesser extent in an attempt to publicize particular landscapes. It has also been demonstrated that certain producers did not feel represented by particular organizations' portrayals of their region. The example of Northwestern respondents assertion that Northwest Tourism primarily promoted the landscape of Donegal as being representative of the entire region is a case in point. Dissatisfaction among tourism businesses with Ireland West's selection of parts of Galway and Mayo, as well as the Midlands East's extensive use of the landscapes of counties Meath and Wicklow, as being symbolic of their respective regions further illustrates the point (see Chapter 4 for further discussion).

A useful example of how place myths contribute to the organization of meanings in space is illustrated through producers' discussions of whether they felt their region possessed a particular image, and how this image might be improved if necessary. In the Midlands, the majority of respondents felt that their region lacked any image and the main reason cited for this was Bord Fáilte's persistent promotion of the already well known tourist areas, such as Kerry, Galway and Dublin. It was felt that these landscapes became associated with Ireland and "Irishness" abroad and that tourists, therefore, choose these as their holiday destinations before even entering the country. Other reasons which were felt to contribute to this lack of an image in the Midlands included the multiplicity of bodies within the region which led to a fragmented, uncoordinated approach to its promotion, especially in County Offaly, and the lack of initiative on the part of local people to instigate their own development. Of those respondents who felt the region had an image, the vast majority felt it was a negative one. The words used most often to describe this image were 'flat', 'uninteresting' and a place to pass through on the way to somewhere else. Other images associated with the area were bogs, Bord na Móna[1] and a place of economic depression, again seen as largely negative images.

Producers in the Midlands suggested a number of different ways in which the negative image of the region could be improved. The importance of utilizing the positive aspects of the region, in terms of its uncrowded, uncommercialized, natural environment, was emphasized. In other words, using the very underdeveloped nature of the region as a selling point was seen as a potential strategy; 'not to try to make it like Kerry'. It was felt that consumers' attitudes were changing and that they no longer wanted to visit highly developed tourist regions but instead wanted to see the 'real Ireland that was not laid on for the tourists'. Overall it was felt that the unique and positive aspects of the region needed to be identified, products then developed based on these resources, and marketed in a synchronized manner. Some believed that the facilities and attractions were already in place, but that they were not being promoted effectively, either by Bord Fáilte or the plethora of uncoordinated agencies in the region. One opinion was that, until the Tourist Board promoted the Midlands abroad, the image would remain underdeveloped; 'before [tourists] come in they have their holiday planned – they only know about Clonmacnoise – they come in for a day and then are gone'. Currently, it was believed, that a tourist could 'look up any [web]site/page or any Bord Fáilte book and only see the tourist areas – Kerry, Killarney, Clare'. In addition, I have already pointed out how it was felt that Laois, Offaly and Westmeath suffered because of their inclusion in the Midlands East Tourism region and that Meath and Wicklow received most of this organization's support. It was also believed that the other regional support organizations and local authorities were 'not geared towards tourism the way they are in the Western counties'. Others felt that it was up to small businesses to unite and put together a package for tourists, or to focus on certain strong products, e.g. angling and golf, and market the region in this way. One such recommendation involved producers coming together to achieve a consensus on how to promote the region and then all individuals reinforcing this image; 'the Midlands is undiscovered' was suggested as a theme, another suggestion was to use the unique boglands landscape as a way of raising the profile of the region. For many, however, the belief was that the region was not a tourist area, so 'we have to sell what we have'.

Institutional respondents tended to agree with this negative image with national crafts and tourism organizations being unanimous in the view that the Midlands had the 'worst' image of the three study areas. Multi-sectoral organizations within the region felt that the Midlands had 'not as defined an image as some other regions', describing it as 'nondescript', a 'pass through' region, lacking identity, and with few large, readily identifiable attractions that people would identify. The Midlands regional tourism organizations were somewhat more positive in describing the region in terms that reflected its "quality" attributes: as a special interest destination with unfulfilled potential, particularly for angling and boating. Its underdeveloped, unpolluted, environmentally positive image was seen as a resource to be exploited with the wider Midlands area being described as 'an unexplored oasis', with South Offaly being viewed as slightly more developed than the rest of the region. However, in general it was also recognized that there was no tradition of tourism in the area and that it was seen as a place to 'pass through'. Reasons given for the lack of a tourism image were similar to those expressed by producers, namely, Bord Fáilte's policy of only promoting well known areas such as Kerry, and an uncoordinated, fragmented approach to marketing the region.

Organizations were also asked how they felt potential consumers viewed each of the three regions. Again, it was felt by tourism organizations in the Midlands that consumers had very little awareness of the region, other than as an area to pass through, with 'nothing to offer', or as a special interest destination, particularly for angling. Nevertheless, awareness among tour operators was viewed as increasing. These customers were 'very aware of key individual products, but not the whole package'. Multi-sectoral organizations had a very pessimistic view of consumers' and customers' perceptions of the region, feeling they either had no image at all or a negative one; 'Irish people wouldn't consider holidaying in the Midlands'. This negative image of the Midlands is long established. In a survey of secondary school students attitudes to counties in Ireland carried out in the 1970s, Laois, Offaly and Westmeath were among the lowest ranked (Gillmor, 1974).

Another interesting point to note in relation to organizational respondents' views on their regional images was that multi-sectoral organizations in the

Northwest and Southwest tended to discuss only the image of their own county, not the region as a whole. In contrast, those in the Midlands referred to the image of the region, primarily, with only little reference to their respective counties. This may suggest that the counties in the other two regions were seen to have distinct identities, whereas the Midlands counties were perceived to have little to distinguish them.

In contrast to the Midlands, in the Northwest, most of the respondents described the image of the region in positive terms. The minority of negative responses primarily related to the absence of a specific regional image: like the Midlands, it was also seen as a place that people passed through, or did not even know existed. The reason given for this lack of an image was an absence of promotion, again by Bord Fáilte and the regional tourism authority, and also poor organization of the tourist industry in the area. Some saw it as having a negative, backward, poor image and an association with the civil unrest in Northern Ireland. The positive images related to the unspoiled, uncrowded landscape, beautiful scenery, the opportunities for leisure, particularly water-based activities, and rurality. The cultural/historical aspect was also important, especially the Yeats connection in Sligo. Distinguishing features of the region cited included: a wealth of archaeological and historical sites such as Carrowmore, Knocknarea, Boyle Abbey, Strokestown House and Clonalis House, beautiful scenery, an unspoiled landscape, the sea, beaches, lakes and mountains such as Ben Bulben, rurality and traditional music.

In the Northwest, the suggestion most frequently mentioned by craftworkers to improve the image of the region was similar to that of tourism respondents in the Midlands, i.e. increased promotion of the region by Bord Fáilte, as it was felt that it had 'never been marketed by any body effectively' and that this was 'a Tourist Board issue'. In relation to Northwest Tourism it was felt that if counties other than Donegal received due promotion, the image of the study region could be enhanced. Developing the tourism product by adding facilities and effecting environmental improvements was also cited. It was indicated that the Leitrim County Enterprise Board's *Visual Leitrim* programme was attempting to improve the image of the area by promoting 'an artistic, entrepreneurial image' and 'highlighting the fact that there are entrepreneurs who produce quality products' in the county. Concern was expressed by a small number of respondents that the image of the region should not be developed further, reflecting the concern expressed in the Midlands that the area may become over-commercialized by the tourism industry. It was felt that developing the regional image too much 'could be dangerous' as it was possible to 'destroy something with too many tourists'. As in the Midlands, a number of respondents felt that producers should band together to market the area.

Institutional respondents viewed the Northwest as being further along the path of image development than the Midlands, but with work still to do. National tourism organizations saw the region as being unspoiled and remote, with potential for tourism, but as yet not well known. It was described as a region 'for people who want to get away from it all', as providing 'a unique and traditional rural experience', with a good product, low population density and lack of traffic congestion, natural beauty and friendly people, and 'not a typical tourist destination'. At a sub-regional level, Roscommon was described as trying to create an image, with heritage and culture as its main selling point. It also had a good activity base, a high quality product and friendly people, but lacked hotel accommodation and wet weather facilities, and was undersold by the marketing bodies. Sligo was seen as being scenic and tranquil with a good angling product that was under-utilized. The region as a whole was described in terms of its unspoiled environment and strong cultural identity. Regarding consumers' images of the region, it was felt that a more positive image existed than that described in relation to the Midlands, however, some negative responses were also recorded. These were largely to do with the region's perceived proximity to Northern Ireland and the 'troubles'. Also, some respondents felt that the image overall was underdeveloped and that the region was seen as primarily as remote and disadvantaged.

Not surprisingly, in relation to the Southwest, the vast majority of respondents saw their region as having a positive image, which was described in terms of the natural, scenic beauty, the rural, unspoilt and uncrowded nature of the landscape, the friendly people, the strong Irish culture, particularly in terms of the Gaeltacht and a reputation for good food. The negative image responses related to the over-commercialization of the region. Less than half of the craftworkers in the region felt the place imagery could be improved in any way, 'how can you improve on what's already there'. Of those who felt the image could be enhanced, methods included: marketing the area as a high quality, upmarket destination, not aimed at high quantities of tourists, a 'more conscientious approach to development' in terms of reducing the numbers of hotels and traffic, paying more attention to the cleanliness of the environment, and improving roads. In contrast, most of the tourism entrepreneurs felt that the image of the Southwest could be improved and the methods mentioned reflected some of those identified by craftworkers, namely environmental protection and improvement, curtailment of tourist industry development and improving roads. It was recognized that there was a danger of over-development so it was 'important that the environment is kept natural, important to have good planning', and 'close co-operation between all agencies involved in environmental promotion' was necessary. Litter on beaches, derelict houses, and pollution of rivers and lakes by hotels were problems that needed to be tackled. Overcrowding was seen as another problem which was adding to the degradation of the environment and was attributed primarily to tour operators who 'bring in tours, all paid for already and no money is being spent in the area'.

Predictably, the organizational respondents viewed the Southwest as being the best developed of the three regions. The regional tourism organizations had predominantly positive images of the region, describing it as 'scenically beautiful', with a high quality tourism infrastructure and a clean, unspoiled environment. It was viewed as being 'the best there is ... scenic, historic, it has everything'. It was felt that North Kerry was lagging slightly behind the rest of the county, but that as a result it was more active in promoting itself. All of the national tourism organizations agreed that the Southwest was probably the best developed tourism region in the country, had spectacular scenery and high quality, successful tourism products and that it 'almost sells itself'. They also suggested that the region was becoming a victim of its own success, with overcrowding and a developing image as a mass tourism, over-commercialized destination. Also, in relation to crafts, the region was viewed as being the best developed of the three and reasons included the proximity of Cork city, the richer economy, and the presence of Údarás na Gaeltachta in Kerry, which contributed to this county becoming more active in terms of crafts production, overtaking the crafts image held by West Cork.

Multi-sectoral organizations described Kerry as having a 'vibrant industrial sector', with a high quality environment and way of life on the one hand, and as 'lightly populated, peripheral, deeply rural, suffering the same structural difficulties as every rural area ... [and with] a lack of entrepreneurial activity', on the other. West Cork was seen as being cosmopolitan, upmarket, clean, green, unspoiled with beautiful scenery, friendly people, and an 'extensive array of speciality food products and a gourmet reputation', but also with problems of peripherality, a lack of employment opportunities and infrastructural deficiencies. In general, crafts organizations in the Southwest felt that consumers and customers did not have any regional image, that they saw the products as being Irish or only perceived the image being portrayed by the individual craftsperson. However, it was recognized that because customers had a positive view of the region generally and because of the large numbers of tourists visiting the area, it was to individual businesses advantage to operate from there. Most regional and national tourism organizations and multi-sectoral organizations perceived consumers and customers as sharing their image of the Southwest, i.e. a popular, well-developed, beautiful tourist destination. One local organization diverged somewhat in its view that consumers saw South Kerry as 'overpriced and under-resourced in terms of infrastructure' and that tour operators image of the area was as 'a day-trip from Killarney'.

So, we can see that overall the Midlands was described as having the "worst", and the Southwest the "best", image in terms of both crafts and tourism, with the Northwest falling somewhere in between. Whilst problems similar to those mentioned in the Midlands were identified in the Northwest, both producers and organizations were overwhelmingly more optimistic in the Northwest about the region's future development. Pessimism and negativity were rife in the responses recorded in the Midlands, both in relation to the region's future potential and individual business growth. This relates to Shields (1991) argument that marginal places 'carry the image, and stigma, of their marginality which becomes indistinguishable from any basic empirical identity' (p. 3). Historically the Midlands has developed as peripheral in a cultural classification with Dublin and the East as the "centre" and the West as embodying all that is intrinsically Irish, leaving all those counties in the middle with no clear image or a negative one.

A question arises as a consequence of the contrast between the Midlands and the other two study regions, the proverbial chicken and egg dilemma. It is expected that Bord Fáilte and other national tourism organizations would use the better known, positively perceived images of Ireland in their promotions abroad, as would any product promoter. However, do such organizations promote the well-known areas of Ireland because they are the ones with the most positive image abroad, or do these areas have positive images because they have been promoted for so long? In reality, the answer is a combination of both, along with a range of other factors relating to the physical landscapes of these regions, the ways in which we perceive landscapes, and historical and cultural factors. Images of places develop over long periods of time and, as Shields (1991) has pointed out, once an image is established, it is difficult to change it. This has practical implications for businesses located in places with negative images attached, as can be seen in the pessimism expressed by producers in the Midlands, making it more difficult for them to attempt to change the image. As mentioned previously, Shields' (1991) term 'social spatialisation' describes this social construction of the spatial and the ways in which our perceptions of places 'are central to our everyday conceptions of ourselves and of reality' (p. 7).

An interesting case in point is the way in which landscape artists use regional imagery both to create their product and to promote it. I have chosen an artist located in the Northwest region (Business I) as a working example of how perceived images of place can have tangible consequences. Landscape artists characterized a distinct type of use of regional imagery within the sample, in that the product being sold was an image of the place. As in the case of heritage attractions and golf courses, presenting an image of the product involved displaying an image of the place. However, in relation to paintings, the place itself was not being sold, rather it was an image of an image of the place that was portrayed in promotion.

The respondent in Business I had been working as a full-time artist for 31 years prior to the interview and his work comprised abstract paintings of local boglands and seascapes. The object of his work was 'to end up with a sense of place'. The initial promotion and marketing of this product involved approaching art galleries with a portfolio, catalogue or slides of the work. When the gallery agreed to exhibit the paintings, they provided promotion through receptions, press releases and, more recently, the Internet. When becoming established, most artists exhibited in group shows, but once they had established their reputation, exhibited on their own. At the time of interview, Business I was exhibiting three separate shows every 18 months, primarily in Dublin and London and was attempting to break into an American market, therefore he had achieved a level of success. As well as using local landscape images, local placenames were drawn on in naming the paintings, e.g. 'Ballyconnell, Sligo'. Apart from the catalogues and slides of paintings, promotional materials included invitations to exhibitions and postcards which portrayed samples of his work and the title of the painting. When asked why he decided to use such place images, the respondent replied than 'an artist has to respond to something that moves him – the landscape here moves me to make work'. He also stated that he was 'not concerned about the consumers. I'm concerned about the images moving me and hope the consumer will discover what it is that moves me'. For him, the use of place imagery was very important, 'it moves me to create the product'. This business represented a type of producer who used the landscape as inspiration in producing the product. What was being sold to consumers was, in effect, a place image or, more specifically, the artist's particular view of the place. The use of placenames as titles of the paintings reinforced the importance of the particularity of the place in product production.

Now, we can contrast this artist, who described how the place imagery was very important for him in motivating him to create the product, with two artists located in the Midlands. The former artist was located in the north-west of Ireland, amidst the idealized landscape of the West and all it embodies in myth. Whether consciously or sub-consciously, this may affect the artist's way of seeing the place, as it does the visitor's or the consumer's. Therefore, a question arises as to the extent to which the *perceived* mythology of the landscape of the West of Ireland, rather than the artist's actual surroundings, influenced his choice of inspiration and in specifically naming his paintings. This issue is brought into sharp focus when the case of two landscape artists located in the Midlands is compared to the first case. One artist exclusively used the West of Ireland as his subject, stating that 'the Midlands image won't strike a chord with people, it's too ordinary ... in terms of painting, there's very little attraction'. Whilst the other landscape artist did paint Midlands bog and mountain scenery, he changed the titles to less place specific ones when exhibiting in Dublin and elsewhere outside the region, because 'Irish people have quite a negative image of the Midlands'. The issue then is the extent to which the landscape of the Midlands is intrinsically less inspiring than that of the West, and the extent to which the particular "ways of seeing" the West embedded in its mythology, affect these views in, firstly, creating the product and, then, in consuming it. In other words, the social and cultural construction of the spatial cannot be separated from the ways in which we actually live our lives.

In keeping with the perceived lack of positive imagery associated with the Midlands, only two of the surveyed crafts businesses in this region used regional imagery to any great extent in their promotional materials. Both of these businesses produced products with strong connections to the region: one used local raw materials and the other used regional and Irish images in product design. They also used a larger number of promotional media than any other craftworker in this region. These businesses differed greatly from each other, however, in terms of business development, their products and target markets and their objectives in, and reasons for, using place imagery. The first, Business D, was described in Chapter 6. This business was a cooperative and relatively new, and was attempting to use poetry, the Irish language and textual references emphasizing the age of the materials and the artistry and craftsmanship of the producers to establish the product as the embodiment of Irishness and the Irish landscape, and as a unique piece of Irish Art.

In contrast, Business J was established 25 years prior to the interview by an individual entrepreneur who had worked in a similar enterprise abroad and returned home with his newly developed skills to set up his own business. He received capital assistance from the Industrial Development Authority and the business grew to employ 30 people full-time. This business also produced giftware items, but in batches, rather than the highly individualized pieces created by the previous enterprise. The raw material was imported from Britain and the product was initially produced in a Germanic style, because the owner had acquired the skill in Germany and, for the first few years, his sole source of business was a contract to supply the company he had worked for there. However, in an effort to develop the business, he changed the design to appeal to an Irish-American market, in particular. He approached retailers with samples of the product, attended trade shows and advertised in specialist magazines and newspapers. After 20 years, he decided to further expand the business by establishing a retail outlet and show room and providing guided tours of the factory to allow consumers view the craftspeople at work. The outlet was set up as a separate company and became his largest single customer. In this way he retained all of the mark-up on the product. At the time of interview, 55 percent of his trade was in America, 35 percent in Ireland (including his own outlet) and the remainder in Britain. The majority of his consumers in Ireland were tourists and many of his foreign consumers were of Irish descent.

According to this respondent, use of regional imagery in promotion was incidental and, primarily, a consequence of product design and the target market. The business was named after the local town and this was chosen in an effort to mimic the success of Waterford Crystal. Also, most of his competitors were American and, according to him, they used the name of their locality as their trade names, simply to convey a geographical source. Originally, the owner had considered calling the business after a local lake, Lough Owel, and had developed a logo using a sketch of an owl (although the Irish name, *Uail*, actually means "group" or "flock"). However, given that the product was a gift item, targeted at the same market as products such as Waterford Crystal, the town name was eventually chosen. It was decided to keep the logo in conjunction with the new name.

Much of the place imagery used was in the product design. This was an attempt to appeal to a, primarily, Irish-American and tourist market. The dominant images included Celtic designs, the Claddagh ring motif, shamrocks, images from the Book of Kells, depictions of various Irish and local legends, historical figures, Irish saints, Irish ecclesiastical metalwork, fishermen from the Aran Islands, rural images (traditional turf cutters, donkey and cart with a load of hay or milk churns, cows, old canal barges), Irish sporting images (horseracing, hurling, Gaelic football) and Irish dancers. In catalogues and brochures, photographs of the products were combined with explanatory texts describing the subject of the work: 'The Book of Kells is widely regarded as the most significant manuscript to have emerged from Europe's early Middle Ages', 'Hugh O'Neill, the last of the Celtic Kings, was educated in England …'.

Many of the promotional materials also contained an account of the history of this particular craft in Ireland and described how the 'ancient craft' was made 'in the traditional way in our own workshop by Irish men and women'. A variety of slogans was used on the different promotional materials, relating to the product, '*the supreme gift*', and a tradition of craftwork, '*history in the making*', and in connecting to the place, '*Ireland… past and present*'. In publicizing the retail outlet and guided tours of the factory, the images used were partly drawn from tourism promotion rhetoric and partly from imagery of craftwork and tradition, as discussed above. For example, descriptions such as 'Westmeath, sitting eloquently in the heart of Ireland is the ideal setting for a holiday or short break', combined with a list of local attractions and facilities, would not be out of place in a tourism business's literature. Whilst elsewhere on the same brochure, references to 'ancient crafts', craftsmanship, skill and traditional methods 'often handed down from father to son' connoted authenticity, quality and integrity.

The extent to which each of the businesses was linked to the region of production varied greatly. Business D used raw materials drawn exclusively from a particular natural, Irish landscape, normally associated with the Midlands. These materials, combined with craftsmanship and skill, provided the unique selling point of the product. Business J, on the other hand, used imported raw materials and a skill initially acquired in Germany to produce a product which could be produced anywhere. The principal link to the particular place came with the adoption of the place name as the business name and this was a direct attempt to emulate Waterford Crystal's success in the marketplace.

The products produced by the businesses were very different, and both provide notable, but dissimilar, examples of the use of place imagery in the promotion of crafts products. Business D produced highly individualized, exclusive products which had more in common with fine art sculptures than batch craft items. Images of Celticity, an ancient Irish landscape and "naturalness", combined with marketing methods which added to the exclusivity of the product and added-value packaging and labelling, achieved the required product positioning. Business J produced batch, hand-made gift items aimed at a mass, primarily, Irish-American, British and tourist market. To a certain extent, old-fashioned "Oirish" imagery, comprising shamrocks, Claddagh ring motifs and Celtic patterns, was used to produce almost souvenir type items for these target markets. The development of the place of production as a tourist attraction adds to this concept. However, images of craftsmanship and authenticity were also connoted in an attempt to validate the genuineness of the product and establish it as something more than a common souvenir. In both cases, products depicting a wide range of other Irish images were produced, firmly positioning the product as an Irish one, rather than a regional product. These producers have also tapped into the argument for the continuation of particular place images, where economic benefits can be identified (Hughes, 1998), as have most of the case study businesses examined throughout the book. Business J in particular, along with Business C and the following example, all use stereotypical Irish imagery to promote their product at home and abroad.

Business K was established 11 years prior to the interview when the respondent was made redundant from her previous job, which motivated her to become self-employed. Initial funding was received from the Industrial Development Authority (IDA) for market research and from An Bord Tráchtála (the Irish Trade Board[2]) for export marketing. The products produced were batch gift items and the range expanded over time. According to the respondent the uniqueness of the product derived from the use of Irish imagery in design and the quality of the materials used. The initial research identified a market for this type of product which no-one else was producing at the time. Refinements were made to product design based on feedback received from retail outlets and the range was expanded. Having developed the product, British and American export markets were targeted with An Bord Tráchtála assistance. At the time of interview, a wide range of methods of promotion and marketing was used, including catalogue and brochure distribution, trade fair attendance, direct approach to retail outlets, point of display promotional materials, trade magazines, agents in Dublin, Northern Ireland, Scotland and England, a distributor in the U.S.A. and membership of a national marketing group.

As with Business J above, the imagery used by this producer in product design was primarily Irish and different ranges had different themes, e.g. the Claddagh Collection bore the Claddagh ring motif and the brochure/catalogue described the image, 'The Claddagh Ring comes from the village of Claddagh just outside Galway City ... The hand signifies friendship, the crown, loyalty and the heart, love'. Other Irish motifs such as the shamrock and the flower of the fuchsia plant occurred within other product ranges. Generic countryside scenes were also used, such as country cottages, butterflies and flowers. Whilst specific local (Ben Bulben, The Thistle Collection – 'Reflecting the beautiful hills of the surrounding countryside') and other place (Achill, Connemara scenes, Newgrange swirls) imagery were also present, they were used as signifiers of "Irishness" rather than as denoting the specific place; 'A timeless Irish classic range'.

The Irish language was also used on many of the items, always with an English translation. The use of Irish signifies "Irishness", but because a translation was included, the actual meaning of the words is also signified. The respondent identified these items as being intended for an Irish market, primarily, hence the use of the English translation, which may appear contradictory. As has been shown previously (Chapter 6) when the Irish language is used on its own, it is generally not meant to be understood for its message, it simply signifies "Irishness", therefore it is not necessarily intended for an Irish market. The use of the Irish language in this case identifies the product as being made in Ireland, which the respondent felt was an important selling point as consumers liked 'to buy Irish'.

The name of this business utilized a particular local landscape feature and the logo was composed of fern fronds which grew in profusion in this environment. These images were chosen also as signifiers of Irishness rather than locality; according to the respondent, she personally chose the name and logo because 'it fits into the image of the company I want to portray – a good quality Irish product'. Fern fronds were also included in most of the photographs of the product in brochures/catalogues in an attempt to naturalize the product and connote environmental consciousness and authenticity. Potted plants and vases of cut flowers were frequently present in photographs signifying a genteel, tamed nature which was more in line with the image of the product being portrayed than the wild nature of previous examples (cf. Figures 4.1 and 4.2). The business card and logo of the enterprise were in the colour green with the slogan '*Distinctive Irish* [product]', invoking a recognized colour symbol of Ireland.

This business, and others like it, deliberately chose to include well-known or stereotypical images of Irishness in product design as an attempt to differentiate it from other products in the market and to encourage consumers to buy Irish.

Whilst arguments can be made for the continuation of such an approach where economic benefits accrue, issues arise when meanings of place are contested by disparate social groups who seek to challenge the unproblematic, fixed and so-called authentic identities expounded (Kneafsey, 1995). Also, from a purely economic standpoint, as Gold and Gold (1995) have pointed out in relation to Scottish tourism promotion, any conservative and incomplete portrayal of a place in product promotion may limit the place's ability to broaden its tourist base and, in turn, limit business' ability to broaden their consumer profile.

Notes

1 Bord na Móna is a leading supplier, in Ireland and internationally, of products and services based on peat. Formerly the statutory body responsible for the development and exploitation of Ireland's boglands, Bord na Móna is now a public limited company that owns and develops some 85,000ha of peatlands, mainly in the Midlands of Ireland. Although the primary responsibility of the company was (according to the Turf Development Act of 1946) to develop Ireland's peat resources, a strong commitment to the social and economic development of the Midlands of Ireland was part of the motivation of the company and of its government owners. From the 1950s onwards, the economies of counties such as Offaly became reliant on the peat extraction industry and the associated electricity generating power stations to such an extent that, when a programme of change, down-sizing and divisionalization was begun in 1988 to reduce costs and make the company more market focused, the results were devastating.

2 An Bord Tráchtála merged with Forbairt (the state agency responsible for Research and Development) in 1998 to form Enterprise Ireland. Those producers who had received assistance before this merger took place referred to the separate organizations.

Chapter 9

Conclusion

It is increasingly recognized that tourism promotional bodies contribute greatly to the creation of the imagined geographies of places abroad (O'Connor, 1993; Gold and Gold, 1995; Waitt, 1997; Markwick, 2001). In this context, research has been conducted on national bodies' promotions of Ireland as a tourism destination. However, to date, little has been done at a regional or local level to examine the creation of more micro-place specific images by individual tourism providers or other businesses, such as hand crafts producers. Also the extent to which the two industries borrow from, and feed into, firstly each other, and secondly, macro place myths and iconographies, is under explored. This book addresses, to some degree, this gap that existed in the literature through an investigation of the use of imagery, especially images of place, for the purposes of promotion and marketing by hand crafts and rural tourism SMEs in three contrasting regions in the Republic of Ireland. The selection of quality products, and of contrasting regions, was deliberate so as to identify examples of best practice, and of the contrasts, if any, that may exist between different geographical contexts. Through a socio-semiotic analysis of promotional materials used by both producers of quality products and their support organisations, I have highlighted the role of place (particularly, rural) imagery in the promotion of individual products and services in Ireland; stressed some of the critical issues concerning the development and application of these images; and suggested some of the meanings which may be connotated through the use of such imagery. In this concluding chapter, I summarize the findings of the research in the context of three related themes. Firstly, I will discuss the methods and processes of place image creation and promotion as identified by the surveyed businesses and organisations. Secondly, I will present an overview of the imagery used and the possible meanings signified. Finally, I will discuss some of the implications of these findings, both for users and promoters of place imagery and the wider society.

The Method

One of the objectives of this book was to determine the methods employed by producers and organizations to use links to place and regional imagery in the promotion of crafts and rural tourism. The organizations surveyed used regional images in a variety of ways in their own promotional work and also supported producers in their use of imagery. Examples of the use of regional labels in text (e.g. *Visual Leitrim*) and image (e.g. Children of Lir symbol) formats and a combination of both (e.g. "*West Cork – A place apart*" with the *Fuchsia* logo) were represented in each region. More general applications of imagery included use of specific regional features and attractions, location maps, and generic rural, coastal, landscape and people images, in text, photographic and illustrative formats. Such imagery was used in guidebooks, brochures, letterheads, videos, advertisements and display stands. Descriptive slogans were often used in conjunction with the images. Most of the organizations in the Midlands and Northwest were attempting to create a new image, or change a negative one, for their respective regions, whilst those in the Southwest tended to use the well-established, recognized images that existed. Methods of supporting producers' use of imagery included providing manuals to assist the use of the various brands, support in brochure and catalogue production, advice, and facilitating contacts with designers.

A majority of the businesses surveyed used some form of regional imagery in their product promotion and most of these used local imagery, although a number of craftworkers used generic Irish images. Whilst a local or regional place name or other place image was used in their product name by only a small proportion of craftspeople, many craftworkers drew on regional images (either actual features or stylized images) in their product design. A number of crafts respondents were also linked to the place of production through use of regional raw materials and this feature was used in promotion. Craftworkers also used regional images on packaging, brochures, labels, swing tags and logos. In general, place imagery was used by crafts producers in an effort to classify the product as being Irish or locally made, to highlight the use of indigenous, natural raw materials and, in the case of the Southwest, to tap into existing positive images of the area. Most craftspeople felt regional imagery had had a positive impact on the success of their product.

Tourism respondents in the three regions often used place names in their product name, in conjunction with physical or cultural features which were employed to convey an attractive image of the area. After the product name, brochures were the most commonly used method of portraying regional imagery. Most of the tourism businesses used similar types of images including actual regional attractions; generic and specific images of activities available locally; historical, literary and artistic figures and events associated with the region; and, generic coastal, mountain, bog and lake scenery. Images were portrayed in photographs, drawings and text. Other promotional tools using regional imagery included business logos, merchandise, the Internet, advertisements and producer marketing groups. Most tourism entrepreneurs used regional images to convey an impression of the region as a good place to take a holiday, emphasizing the beauty of the scenery, amenities, the quality of the food, country house comfort and the peacefulness of the area. In the Midlands such imagery was also used to overcome negative images that were felt to exist, whilst in the Southwest respondents highlighted an attempt to tap into consumers' pre-existing positive ideas about the region. Most also felt that using regional imagery had had a positive impact on business success. However, respondents in the Midlands were less convinced about the impact of the use of place imagery than those in the other two regions.

Throughout the book, case studies were used to illustrate the range of ways in which links to place and place imagery may be utilized in the promotion of crafts and rural tourism. Selected crafts producers in the Midlands exploited links to place through the use of specifically local or Irish raw materials and craftsmanship and the use of images of place in product design. The imagery adopted by Business D arose from the use of natural, Irish raw materials drawn from the Midlands landscape as the unique selling point of the product. Imagery reflecting the atmosphere of this landscape, "naturalness" and "Irishness" were combined to position the product as the embodiment of Irish artwork. Business J, on the other hand, used generic and specific Irish imagery in an effort to appeal to the target market chosen for the product. The product itself had no links to the region and a place name was chosen to imitate the well-known Waterford Crystal. The tourism businesses in this region represented enterprises with strong place connections, one product being part of the heritage of the place (Business E) and the other being part of the landscape itself, with the terrain providing a unique setting for the product (Business F).

In the Northwest, the selected crafts producers exemplified the use of local and Irish place names as product titles or brand names to create market differentiation and to distinguish the craft as being Irish made (Business K), and also reflected the use of landscape as artistic inspiration (Business I). The second example demonstrated the way in which place, either real or imagined, may be used as artistic inspiration so that a particular view of the location, that of the artist, is presented for consumption. The two tourism businesses selected in this region used imagery in similar ways, in that recognized aspects of the place imagery of County Sligo were evoked in order to create a distinct atmosphere for the products, one of a fantastic land steeped in heritage and mythology (Businesses A and B).

The crafts business featured in the Southwest (Business C) provided a particularly good example of the successful use of place imagery in a conscious and co-ordinated way throughout a range of promotional materials. The deliberate use of certain Irish and local images in product design and promotion positioned the products as representing "Irishness" in export markets and has placed this business as a market leader in the craft category. The selected tourism respondents illustrated the way in which some businesses promote their particular locations as well as their product: to highlight the advantages of the landscape for the product being promoted (Business G), and to tap into a pre-existing positive perception of the specific location (Business H). The case studies provide examples of "best practice" in the use of place imagery as a marketing device, as all are successful businesses who identified the use of connections to place as a significant element in this success.

The Imagery Used

Tourism promotion generates imagined geographies of places (Waitt, 1997) and is one of the principal ways in which a place is represented to outsiders (Gold and Gold, 1995). It has been argued that "Tourism is important to geographers ... for its semiotic realization of the spaces that are nurtured in the tourist's imagination" (Hughes, 1998, p. 30). As I have already discussed, it is my contention that it is not only tourism promotional bodies which generate geographies of place, but any organization, business or individual that uses place imagery to communicate a promotional message. Therefore, another objective of this book was to categorize and analyze the content of promotional materials used by small businesses of both rural tourism and hand crafts services and products. This analysis demonstrated the predominance of brochures or flyers as the medium of choice among such businesses, followed by business cards, web pages and swing tags or labels. In fact, many respondents were represented in more than one medium. Approval symbols, logos, maps, photographs, sketches, slogans and text were identified as the units of content within the media, with textual and photographic images being most prevalent overall. A range of connotated myths symbolized in the particularly imagery chosen was identified using a simple socio-semiotic analysis.

Several recurring themes were identified which were used in a variety of ways to promote these products. Apart from providing practical information about the product, themes related to "connection to place/use of regional imagery", "people", "craftsmanship and tradition", "landscape/natural environment", "connecting with the past", "praise/characteristics of the product", "tranquillity", "invitation to consumers" and "rurality". Whilst the use of connection to place and specific regional imagery was prevalent in both sectors and in the three regions, it was particularly common among craftworkers in the Southwest (in photographs and text) and among tourism providers in the Midlands (in text). In the Southwest, craftworkers used such imagery to tap into, particularly tourists', established images of this region, whilst in the Midlands, tourism providers used images of the place to inform readers of the various attractions available in a relatively unknown region.

Tourism respondents used various images of people, ranging from depictions of members of the target market enjoying relevant activities, to proprietors and employees of the business, signifying hospitality and a friendly service. For craftworkers, descriptions of craftsmanship and skill and a long tradition of craftwork were recurring themes, especially in relation to the handmade production of the products, connoting authenticity and quality. Images of nature and the environment, as well as evocations of the past, tapped into myths of the countryside idyll, harmony with nature and the pleasures and simplicity of past times.

Overall, the image portrayed was one of a natural, unspoiled, peaceful and rural environment, where traditional methods of production survive in an idealized landscape out of time. The common message was one of invitation to experience the tranquillity of the countryside and to escape from the modern, urban experience through consumption of its products (crafts) and the place itself (rural tourism).

The Implications

In the Introduction I highlighted the fact that representations of the rural can have practical impacts in numerous ways. An important impact, as identified by Ward (1998, p. 239), is that 'Once created ... promotional messages are partly liberated from their primary discourse of selling ... [becoming] part of more widely accepted ideals about places'. One of the issues discussed during the conduct of this research was the images held by producers and organizations of the three study regions. Overall, the Midlands was seen as having no image, or a negative one, which was attributed in part to a lack of promotion of the region by organizations at local, regional and national level. As discussed in Chapter 8, negative descriptions of the region included being "flat", uninteresting, underdeveloped, economically depressed and not a tourist area, but a place to pass through on the way to somewhere else. The images of the Northwest identified were somewhat more positive than those of the Midlands. Organizations and producers in this region appeared to have been through the process of identifying the unique strengths of the area and were attempting to turn the negative aspects of remoteness, underdevelopment and isolation into a more positive image of a 'wild and wonderful West', with an emphasis on culture and heritage. To a certain degree, the image was constructed in opposition to the better/(over) developed tourist areas of Ireland. The Southwest had the image that was perceived as being most widely recognized. Positive landscape, cultural, and culinary images were identified and the overarching image was that of a scenically beautiful tourist region, with a highly advanced tourist infrastructure and attractions. However, it was felt that this traditional view of the region was being infiltrated by a new image of a mass tourism destination, with the associated problems of overcrowding, traffic congestion and environmental degradation.

The implications for regions with associations of negative or positive imagery is that place promotion propagates such images. They become part of 'a larger network of circulated ideas about the nature of place' (Johnson, 2000, p. 260), both in the images used in promotional materials and in the attitudes of organizations involved in the promotion or otherwise of place imagery as a marketing tool. This can lead to ongoing negative associations which have wider implications for people settling in these areas, as well as for economic and social development in general. Ongoing positive associations, regardless of the reality, can result in greater tourist numbers to such areas, thus spoiling the place in contradiction to the image. Also place marketing creates unreal expectations about places through use of these emotionally powerful positive associations. Those responsible for place promotion need to attempt to portray more inclusive representations which more accurately signify the 'deeper meanings of place' (Ward, 1998, p. 240). A more comprehensive understanding of the processes, both deliberate and non-deliberate, of image production, communication and consumption is necessary in order to move beyond stereotyped images of places.

As discussed in Chapter 4, it is only relatively recently that rural regions have begun to develop, image and promote themselves in a deliberate and integrated way, primarily for tourism (Butler and Hall, 1998; Mitchell, 1998). I have identified that support organizations can assist producers in developing such marketing strategies, through their own promotional work and in supporting producers in their use of imagery. It was not within the scope of the current research to investigate in any depth the effectiveness or otherwise of organizations' attempts to develop and manage regional branding initiatives. However, some tentative suggestions can be made which may form the bases for further research.

The development of quality branding in the tourism and crafts sectors by West Cork LEADER and Leitrim County Enterprise Board, respectively, illustrated a growing appreciation of the value of a quality and regional designation as a form of market differentiation. These initiatives provide possible models that might be adapted to different circumstances by other sub-regional groups as a means of enhancing the competitiveness of products and services. A crucial aspect of both of these initiatives was the emphasis on quality. However, during interviewing an inconsistency was identified between the way in which the selected organizations and producers defined quality. From the organizations' points of view, quality involved meeting consumer/customer requirements and meeting regulatory standards. These standards, as set by Bord Fáilte in relation to tourism, were viewed as being less than adequate by the producers. Most multi-sectoral organizations relied on sectoral agencies' definitions of quality, thus augmenting this discrepancy between producers and organizations. This lack of sympathy between the interests of organizations and producers suggests that appropriate strategies need to be adopted to support small scale quality businesses who are interested in developing commercial enterprises. Consultation with producers on additional quality regulations for certain niche products and allocating additional resources to SMEs in particular, are suggested ways forward.

On a related point, numerous product marketing groups were identified, particularly in the tourism sector. However, the existence of effective national sectoral groups may hamper the development of regional groups, as membership of one group may prohibit membership of any other. State and regional organizations need to ensure that the standards they adopt in developing quality branding are sufficiently high and rigorously implemented to attract high quality businesses.

In relation to organizations which are already engaged in regional branding and utilization of place imagery in product promotion, dissatisfaction was expressed by a number of producers with the images used by certain organizations. At regional level, tourism respondents in the Midlands and Northwest felt less than represented by their Regional Tourism Authorities. It was believed that these organizations concentrated on promoting the already well-developed tourist locales in their regions (Donegal – Northwest Tourism, parts of Galway and Mayo – Ireland West, Meath and Wicklow – Midlands East Tourism), utilizing imagery from these areas to represent the region as a whole. Also, at a local level, some respondents in the Ely O'Carroll area felt that this image was not representative of South Offaly, having more connections with North Tipperary. Organizations need to be aware of these issues in developing regional labels, to ensure that the images used are representative of the entire region, not just specific sections. Consultation with businesses prior to developing such imagery could lead to a more inclusive representation of the region in promotion and also give producers ownership of the process. This may better persuade businesses to adopt the images recommended.

Finally, some lessons may be learned from the case studies illustrated in relation to the best way to utilize connections to place/regional imagery in product promotion. The selected case studies appear to have a number of common features. First of all, identification of what it is about the product which makes it unique to the place seems to be important. Several exemplars were identified: the use of local raw materials, craftsmanship or local/place imagery in product design, the physical location of the business in terms of terrain and environment, the historical connections of the product to the place, the use of local place names as product titles or brand names, the landscape as artistic inspiration, and the selection of particular aspects of place imagery to create a certain mood or atmosphere for the product. Other examples included the use of Irish imagery in product design and promotion to position products as representing "Irishness" in export markets, utilizing place imagery to sell the particular location as well as the product or simply using the existing images of a well known place to promote the product. Having identified the connections between the product and the place, the next step is to plan and implement a deliberate and co-ordinated approach to promoting this connection. All aspects of product promotion, from advertisements to logos, and from packaging to personal selling, need to emphasize the same message. In this way, the product will be associated with the place and will come to embody the place characteristics in the minds of consumers, and vice versa. For this reason, the most important element in the imaging process is the adherence to strict quality standards in all aspects of the business, including raw materials, production, service delivery and promotion. In this way, the area comes to be identified as a locale for quality products and, in turn, the product is associated with the quality of the place.

Although this work is grounded in Irish examples, the underpinning concepts, methods and results are transferable across rural spaces in general, but particularly in an ever-expanding European Union. In many ways the Irish experience provides an ideal exemplar for highlighting these conceptions and, undoubtedly, other European countries can benefit from Ireland's accomplishments in the areas of rural development and rural tourism. In particular, it has been identified that developing branding or "identities" for rural tourism destinations can help position these regions in an increasingly competitive international marketplace (WTO, 2002). This book highlights some of the theoretical underpinnings of such a marketing approach.

Bibliography

Adler, J. (1989), 'Origins of sightseeing', *Annals of Tourism Research*, Vol. 16 (1), pp. 7-29.

Aitken, S. C. (1997), 'Analysis of texts: armchair theory and couch-potato geography', in R. Flowerdew and D. Martin (eds.), *Methods in human geography*, Longman, Essex, pp. 197-212.

Ashworth, G. J. and Voogd, H. (1990), *Selling the city: marketing approaches in public sector urban planning*, Belhaven Press, London.

Ashworth, G. J. and Voogd, H. (1994), 'Marketing and place promotion', in J. R. Gold and S. V. Ward (eds.), *Place promotion: the use of publicity and marketing to sell towns and regions*, Wiley, Chichester, pp. 39-52.

Azaryahu, M. and Kellerman, A. (1999), 'Symbolic places of national history and revival: a study in Zionist mythical geography', *Transactions of the Institute of British Geographers*, Vol. 24 (1), pp. 109-23.

Barham, E. (2003), 'Translating terroir: the global challenge of French AOC labeling', *Journal of Rural Studies*, Vol. 19 (1), pp. 127-38.

Barke, M. and Harrop, K. (1994), 'Selling the industrial town: identity, image and illusion', in J. R. Gold and S. V. Ward (eds.), *Place promotion: the use of publicity and marketing to sell towns and regions*, Wiley, Chichester, pp. 93-114.

Barrington, T. J. (1976), *Discovering Kerry*, Blackwater, Dublin.

Barthes, R. (1973), *Mythologies*, Paladin, London.

Barthes, R. (1977), *Image Music Text*, Fontana Press, London.

Bastin, R. (1985), 'Participant observation in social analysis', in R. Walker (ed.), *Applied qualitative research*, Gower, Aldershot, pp. 92-100.

Bell, D. (1995), 'Picturing the landscape: *Die Grune Insel*: tourist images of Ireland', *European Journal of Communication*, Vol. 10 (1), pp. 41-62.

Bell, D. and Valentine, G. (1997), *Consuming geographies: we are where we eat*, Routledge, London.

Berger, J. (1972), *Ways of seeing*, Penguin, London.

Bessière, J. (1998), 'Local development and heritage: traditional food and cuisine as tourist attractions in rural areas', *Sociologia Ruralis*, Vol. 38 (1), pp. 21-33.

Blonsky, M. (ed.), (1985), *On signs: a semiotics reader*, Basil Blackwell, Oxford.

Bord Fáilte (1994), *Developing sustainable tourism*, Bord Fáilte, Dublin.

Bord Fáilte (1996a), 'Irish tourism industry launches dramatic new marketing strategy', Press release, 11th November.

Bord Fáilte (1996b), *Investing in strategic marketing for tourism*, Bord Fáilte, Dublin.

Bord Fáilte (1996c), *Link*, Bord Fáilte, Dublin.

Bord Fáilte (1997), *Perspectives on Irish tourism, 1991-1995, the product*, Bord Fáilte, Dublin.

Brett, D. (1994), 'The representation of culture', in U. Kockel (ed.), *Culture, tourism and development: the case of Ireland*, Liverpool University Press, Liverpool, pp. 117-28.

Briggs, S. (1997), *Successful tourism marketing: a practical handbook*, Kogan Page, London.

Brouwer, R. (1997), 'Toerisme en de symbolische toe-eigening van rurale hulpbronnen', *Tijdschnift voor Sociaal-wetenschappelijle onder-zock van de Landbouw*, Vol. 12 (3), pp. 281-305.

Bunce, M. (1994), *The countryside ideal: Anglo-American images of landscape*, Routledge, London.

Burgess, J. (1982), 'Selling places: environmental images for the executive', *Regional Studies*, Vol. 16 (1), pp. 1-17.

Burgess, J. (1985), 'News from nowhere: the press, the riots and the myth of the inner city', in J. Burgess and J. R. Gold (eds.), *Geography, the media and popular culture*, Croom Helm, London, pp. 192-228.

Burgess, J. and Wood, P. (1988), 'Decoding Docklands: place advertising and decision-making strategies of the small firm', in J. Eyles and D. M. Smith (eds.), *Qualitative methods in human geography*, Polity Press, Cambridge, pp. 94-117.

Burgin, V. (1982), 'Photographic practice and art theory', in V. Burgin (ed.), *Thinking photography*, Macmillan, London, pp. 39-83.

Butler, R. W. and Hall, C. M. (1998), 'Image and reimaging of rural areas', in R. Butler, C. M. Hall and J. Jenkins (eds.), *Tourism and recreation in rural areas*, Wiley, Chichester, pp. 116-22.

Buttimer, A. and Seamon, D. (eds.), (1980), *The human experience of space and place*, Croom Helm, London.

Byrne, A., Edmondson, R. and Fahy, K. (1993), 'Rural tourism and cultural identity in the West of Ireland', in B. O'Connor and M. Cronin (eds.), *Tourism in Ireland: a critical analysis*, Cork University Press, Cork, pp. 233-57.

Cawley, M. E., Gaffey, S. and Gillmor, D. A. (1999), 'Regulation and re-regulation in Irish rural tourism', Paper presented to the IGU Commission on the Sustainability of Rural Systems, Simon Fraser University, British Columbia, July.

de Certeau, M. (1984), *The practice of everyday life*, trans. S. Rendell, University of California Press, Berkeley.

Chandler, D. (2000), 'Semiotics for beginners: intertextuality', *http://www.aber.ac.uk/media/Documents/S4B/sem09.html.*

Chapman, M. (1992), *The Celts: the construction of a myth*, MacMillan, London.

Cloke, P. and Little, J. (eds.), (1997), *Contested countryside cultures: otherness, marginalisation and rurality*, Routledge, London.

Commission of the European Communities (1996), *CdR 54/96 Opinion of the Committee of the Regions of 18 September 1996 on promoting and protecting local products – a trump card for the regions*, Commission of the European Communities, Brussels.

Connolly, S. J. (1997), 'Culture, identity and tradition: changing definitions of Irishness', in B. Graham (ed.), *In search of Ireland: a cultural geography*, Routledge, London, pp. 43-63.

Copus, A. (1996), *A rural development typology of European NUTS III regions*, Working Paper 14, AIR3-CT94-1545, *The impact of public institutions on lagging rural and coastal regions*, Scottish Agricultural College, Aberdeen.

Corbett, E. P. J. (1971), *Classical rhetoric for the modern student*, Oxford University Press, New York.

Cosgrove, D. (1984), *Social formation and symbolic landscape*, Croom Helm, London.

Cosgrove, D. (1998), 'Cultural landscapes', in T. Unwin (ed.), *A European geography*, Longman, United Kingdom, pp. 65-81.

Cotter, A. (1992), '"Green" image and marketing – Irish beef', in J. Feehan (ed.), *Environment and development in Ireland*, The Environmental Institute, University College Dublin, Dublin, pp. 179-81.

Cowan, C. and Sexton, R. (1997), *Ireland's traditional foods*, Teagasc, Dublin.

Crang, M. (1998), *Cultural geography*, Routledge, London.

Culler, J. (1988), *Framing the sign: criticism and its institutions*, Basil Blackwell, Oxford.

Dann, G. (1996), 'The people of tourist brochures', in T. Selwyn (ed.), *The tourist image: myths and myth making in tourism*, Wiley, Chichester, pp. 61-81.

Dawson, P. (1994), *Total quality management*, Oxford University Press, Oxford.

Dear, M. and Flusty, S. (1999), 'The postmodern urban condition', in M. Featherstone and S. Lash (eds.), *Spaces of culture: city – nation – world*, Sage, London, pp. 64-85.

Delaney, F. (1993), *The Celts*, Hammersmith, London.

Deleuze, G. (1988), *Foucault*, University of Minnesota Press, Minneapolis.

Denscombe, M. (1998), *The good research guide for small-scale social research projects*, Open University Press, Buckingham.

Denzin, N. K. and Lincoln, Y. S. (eds.), (1994), 'Introduction: entering the field of qualitative research', in *Handbook of qualitative research*, Sage, London, pp. 1-17.

Dibb, S., Simkin, L., Pride, W. M. and Ferrell, O. C. (1991), *Marketing concepts and strategies*, Houghton Mifflin Company, Boston.

Dilley, R. S. (1986), 'Tourist brochures and tourist images', *The Canadian Geographer*, Vol. 30 (1), pp. 59-65.

Dillon, M. (1994), *Early Irish literature*, Four Courts Press, Dublin.

Doswell, R. and Gamble, P. R. (1979), *Marketing and planning hotels and tourism projects*, Hutchinson, London.

Drummery, M. (1992), 'The green image and marketing', in J. Feehan (ed.), *Environment and development in Ireland*, The Environmental Institute, University College Dublin, Dublin, pp. 176-8.

Duffy, P. J. (1994), 'The changing rural landscape 1750-1850: pictorial evidence', in R. Gillespie and B. P. Kennedy (eds.), *Ireland: art into history*, Town House, Dublin, pp. 26-42.

Duffy, P. J. (1997), 'Writing Ireland: literature and art in the representation of Irish place', in B. Graham (ed.), *In search of Ireland: a cultural geography*, Routledge, London, pp. 64-83.

Duncan, J. S. (1990), *The city as text: the politics of landscape interpretation in the Kandyan Kingdom*, Cambridge University Press, Cambridge.

Eco, U. (1976), *A theory of semiotics*, Indiana University Press, Bloomington.

Eco, U. (1982), 'Critique of the image', in V. Burgin (ed.), *Thinking photography*, Macmillan, London, pp. 32-8.

Excellence Ireland (1997), A new vision for the future: information brochure, Excellence Ireland, Dublin.

Fahey, G. (1992), 'The green image: marketing Irish butter' in J. Feehan (ed.), *Environment and development in Ireland*, The Environmental Institute, University College Dublin, Dublin, pp. 182-4.

Fine, B. (1995), 'From political economy to consumption', in D. Miller (ed.), *Acknowledging consumption: a review of new studies*, Routledge, London, pp. 127-63.

Fisher, C. (1997), ''I bought my first saw with my maternity benefit': craft production in west Wales and the home as the space of (re)production', in P. Cloke and J. Little (eds.), *Contested countryside cultures: otherness, marginalisation and rurality*, Routledge, London, pp. 232-51.

Fiske, J. (1990), *Introduction to communication studies*, Routledge, London.

Fleming, D. K. and Roth, R. (1991), 'Place in advertising', *The Geographical Review*, Vol. 81 (3), pp. 281-91.

Geoghegan, E. (1998-2000), 'Heraldic symbolism and convention', *http://homepage.tinet.ie/~donnaweb/heraldry/index.html*.

Gibbons, L. (1996), *Transformations in Irish culture*, Cork University Press, Cork.

Gibson, A. and Nielsen, M. (2000), *Tourism and hospitality marketing in Ireland*, Gill and MacMillan, Dublin.

Gillmor, D. A. (1974), 'Mental maps in geographic education: spatial preferences of some Leinster school leavers', *Geographical Viewpoint*, Vol. 3, pp. 46-66.

Gold, J. R. (1994), 'Locating the message: place promotion as image communication', in J. R. Gold and S. V. Ward (eds.), *Place promotion: the use of publicity and marketing to sell towns and regions*, Wiley, Chichester, pp. 19-37.

Gold, J. R. and Gold, M. M. (1995), *Imagining Scotland: tradition, representation and promotion in Scottish tourism since 1750*, Scolar Press, Aldershot.

Gold, J. R. and Ward, S. V. (eds.), (1994), *Place promotion: the use of publicity and marketing to sell towns and regions*, Wiley, Chichester.

Gottdiener, M. (1995), *Postmodern semiotics: material culture and the forms of postmodern life*, Basil Blackwell, Cambridge.

Goulding, C. (2000), 'The commodification of the past, postmodern pastiche, and the search for authentic experiences at contemporary heritage attractions', *European Journal of Marketing*, Vol. 34 (7), pp. 835-53.

Government of Ireland (1997), *Report of the rural development policy advisory group*, Stationery Office, Dublin.

Government of Ireland (1999), *National development plan 2000-2006*, Stationery Office, Dublin.

Graham, B. (1997), 'Ireland and Irishness: place, culture and identity', in B. Graham (ed.), *In search of Ireland: a cultural geography*, Routledge, London, pp. 1-15.

Graham, B. (2000), 'The past in place: historical geographies of identity', in B. Graham and C. Nash (eds.), *Modern historical geographies*, Pearson Education, Essex, pp. 70-99.

Graham, C. (2001), '"Blame it on Maureen O'Hara": Ireland and the trope of authenticity', *Cultural Studies*, Vol. 15 (1), pp. 58-75.

Gruffudd, P. (1994), 'Back to the land: historiography, rurality and the nation in interwar Wales', *Transactions of the Institute of British Geographers*, Vol. 19 (1), pp. 61-77.

Guerry, P. (1995), 'The linkage between niche products and territory', in OECD (ed.), *Niche markets and rural development: workshop proceedings and policy recommendations*, OECD, Paris, pp. 67-79.

Guetzkow, H. H. (1950), 'Unitizing and categorizing problems in coding qualitative data', *Journal of Clinical Psychology*, Vol. 6, pp. 47-58.

Haartsen, T., Groote, P. and Huigen, P. (2003), 'Measuring age differentials in representations of rurality in The Netherlands', *Journal of Rural Studies*, Vol. 19 (2), pp. 245-52.

Halfacree, K. H. (1993), 'Locality and social representation: space, discourse and alternative definitions of the rural', *Journal of Rural Studies*, Vol. 9 (1), pp. 23-37.

Halfacree, K. H. (1995), 'Talking about rurality: social representations of the rural as expressed by residents of six English parishes', *Journal of Rural Studies*, Vol. 11 (1), pp. 1-20.

Hall and Hall, S. (1841), *Ireland: its scenery and character*, Jeremiah Howe, London.

Heaney, M. (1994), *Over nine waves: a book of Irish legends*, Faber and Faber, London.

Hopkins, J. (1998), 'Signs of the post-rural: marketing myths of a symbolic countryside', *Geografiska Annaler*, Vol. 80 B (2), pp. 65-81.

Hughes, G. (1992), 'Tourism and the geographical imagination', *Leisure Studies*, Vol. 11, pp. 31-42.

Hughes, G. (1998), 'The semiological realization of space', in G. Ringer (ed.), *Destinations: cultural landscapes of tourism*, Routledge, London, pp. 17-32.

Ilbery, B. and Kneafsey, M. (1997), 'Regional images and the promotion of quality products and services in the lagging regions of the European Union', Paper presented to the Third Anglo-French Rural Geography Symposium, Nantes, September.

Ilbery, B. and Kneafsey, M. (1998), 'Product and place: promoting quality products and services in the lagging regions of the European Union', *European Urban and Regional Studies*, Vol. 5 (4), pp. 329-41.

Ilbery, B. and Kneafsey, M. (2000), 'Producer constructions of quality in regional speciality food production: a case study from south west England', *Journal of Rural Studies*, Vol. 16 (2), pp. 217-30.

Ilbery, B., Kneafsey, M., Bowler, I. and Clark, G. (1999), 'Quality products and services in the lagging rural regions of the European Union: a producer perspective', Paper presented to the Rural Geography Symposium, Nova Scotia, July.

Jackson, P. (1999), 'Commodity cultures: the traffic in things', *Transactions of the Institute of British Geographers*, Vol. 24 (1), pp. 95-108.

Jackson, P. and Taylor, J. (1996), 'Geography and the cultural politics of advertising', *Progress in Human Geography*, Vol. 20 (3), pp. 356-71.

Jackson, P. and Thrift, N. (1995), 'Geographies of consumption', in D. Miller (ed.), *Acknowledging consumption: a review of new studies*, Routledge, London, pp. 204-37.

Jakobson, R. and Halle, M. (1956), *The fundamentals of language*, Mouton, The Hague.

Johnson, N. C. (2000), 'Historical geographies of the present', in B. Graham and C. Nash (eds.), *Modern historical geographies*, Pearson Education, Essex, pp. 251-72.

Kalogara, L. S. (1977), *Yeats's Celtic mysteries*, A dissertation submitted to the Department of English in partial fulfilment of the degree of Doctor of Philosophy, The Florida State University, Florida.

Kearney, R. (1988), *Transitions: narratives in modern Irish culture*, Manchester University Press, Manchester.

Kearns, G. and Philo, C. (eds.) (1993), *Selling places: the city as cultural capital, past and present*, Pergamon, Oxford.

Keeble, D., Tyler, P., Broom, G. and Lewis, J. (1992), *Business success in the countryside: the performance of rural enterprises*, HMSO, London.

Kiberd, D. (1995), *Inventing Ireland: the literature of the modern nation*, Johnathan Cape, London.

Kiberd, D. (1996), 'The periphery and the center', *Ireland and Irish Cultural Studies, The South Atlantic Quarterly*, Vol. 95 (1), pp. 5-21.

Kilgannon, E. (1989), *Myths and magic of the Yeats Country*, Mercier Press, Cork.

Kneafsey, M. (1995), 'A landscape of memories: heritage and tourism in Mayo', in U. Kockel (ed.), *Landscape, heritage and identity: case studies in Irish ethnography*, Liverpool University Press, Liverpool, pp. 135-53.

Kneafsey, M. (1997), *Tourism and place identity: change and resistance in the European Celtic periphery*, PhD thesis in Geography, University of Liverpool.

Kockel, U. (1995), '"The West is learning, the North is war": Reflections on Irish identity', in U. Kockel (ed.), *Landscape, heritage and identity: case studies in Irish ethnography*, Liverpool University Press, Liverpool, pp. 237-58.

Kotler, P. (1997), *Marketing management*, Prentice Hall, New Jersey.

Kotler, P. and Zaltman, G. (1971), 'Social marketing: an approach to planned social change', *Journal of Marketing*, July, pp. 3-12.

Kripendorff, K. (1980), *Content analysis: an introduction to its methodology*, Sage, Beverly Hills.

Laenen, M. (1989), 'Looking for the future through the past', in D. Uzzell (ed.), *The natural and built environment*, Vol. 1, Belhaven Press, London, pp. 88-95.

Lagopoulos, A. P. (1993), 'Postmodernism, geography, and the social semiotics of space', *Environment and Planning D*, Vol. 11, pp. 256-78.

Lash, S. (1990), *Sociology of postmodernism*, Routledge, London.

Lash, S. and Urry, J. (1994), *Economies of signs and space*, Sage, London.

Leerssen, J. (1996), *Remembrance and imagination*, Cork University Press, Cork.

Lefebvre, H. (1991), *The production of space*, trans. Nicholson-Smith, D., Basil Blackwell, Oxford.

Leitrim County Enterprise Board (undated), 'Leitrim tempts you to take a closer look', a working guide to assist the consistent application of the brand identity across all media, by all users.

Lévi-Strauss, C. (1966), *The savage mind* (2nd ed.), University of Chicago Press, Chicago.

Littrell, M. A. (1990), 'Symbolic significance of textile crafts for tourists', *Annals of Tourism Research*, Vol. 17 (2), pp. 228-45.

Littrell, M. A., Anderson, L. F. and Brown, P. J. (1993), 'What makes a craft souvenir authentic?', *Annals of Tourism Research*, Vol. 20 (1), pp. 197-215.

Logue, A. (1996), 'Turning over a new leaf', *The Irish Times*, Tuesday, 1 October.

Long, N. (ed.), (1984), *Family and work in rural societies: perspectives on non-wage labour*, Tavistock, London.

Lowenthal, D. (1985), *The past is a foreign country*, Cambridge University Press, Cambridge.

MacCannell, D. (1973), 'Staged authenticity: arrangements of social space in tourist settings', *American Journal of Sociology*, Vol. 79, pp. 589-603.

MacCannell, D. (1976), *The tourist: a new theory of the leisure class*, MacMillan, London.

MacCannell, D. (1989), *The tourist: a new theory of the leisure class*, 2nd ed., MacMillan, London.

MacCannell, D. (1992), *Empty meeting grounds: the tourist papers*, Routledge, London.

Macnaghten, P. and Urry, J. (1998), *Contested natures*, Sage, London.

Marketing Sligo Forum (undated), 'Sligo land of heart's desire', a guide to understanding the brand and working guidelines on how best to assist its consistent application across all media, by all users.

Markwick, M. (2001), 'Marketing myths and the cultural commodification of Ireland: where the grass is always greener', *Geography*, Vol. 86 (1), pp. 37-49.

Marsden, T. (1998), 'New rural territories: regulating the differentiated rural spaces', *Journal of Rural Studies*, Vol. 14 (1), pp. 107-17.

Mason, J. (1994), 'Linking qualitative and quantitative data analysis', in A. Bryman and R. G. Burgess (eds.), *Analyzing qualitative data*, Routledge, London, pp. 89-110.

Mason, J. (1996), *Qualitative researching*, Sage, London.

Maxwell, J. A. (1998), 'Designing a qualitative study', in L. Bickman and D. J. Rog (eds.), *Handbook of applied social research methods*, Sage, London, pp. 69-100.

McIntosh, A. J. and Prentice, R. C. (1999), 'Affirming authenticity: consuming cultural heritage', *Annals of Tourism Research*, Vol. 26 (3), pp. 589-612.

Mellinger, W. M. (1994), 'Toward a critical analysis of tourism representations', *Annals of Tourism Research*, Vol. 21 (4), pp. 756-79.

Middleton, V. T. C. (1994), *Marketing in travel and tourism*, Butterworth-Heinemann, Oxford.

Miele, M. and Murdoch, J. (2002), 'The practical aesthetics of traditional cuisines: slow food in Tuscany', *Sociologia Ruralis*, Vol. 42 (4), pp. 312-28.

Miller, D. (1995), 'Consumption as the vanguard of history: a polemic by way of an introduction', in D. Miller (ed.), *Acknowledging consumption: a review of new studies*, Routledge, London, pp. 1-57.

Milton, K. (1993), 'Land or landscape: rural planning policy and the symbolic construction of the countryside', in M. Murray and J. Greer (eds.), *Rural development in Ireland*, Avebury, Aldershot, pp. 129-50.

Mitchell, C. J. A. (1998), 'Entrepreneurialism, commodification and creative destruction: a model of post-modern community development', *Journal of Rural Studies*, Vol. 14 (3), pp. 273-86.

Morgan, M. (1996), *Marketing for leisure and tourism*, Prentice Hall, London.

Mormont, M. (1990), 'Who is rural? Or, how to be rural: towards a sociology of the rural', in T. Marsden, P. Lowe and S. Whatmore (eds.), *Rural restructuring: global processes and their responses*, Fulton, London, pp. 21-44.

Morris, C. (2000), 'Quality assurance schemes: a new way of delivering environmental benefits in food production?', *Journal of Environmental Planning and Management*, Vol. 43 (3), pp. 433-48.

Murdoch, J. and Pratt, A. C. (1993), 'Rural studies: modernism, postmodernism and the "post-rural"', *Journal of Rural Studies*, Vol. 9 (4), pp. 411-27.

Nash, C. (1993), '"Embodying the nation" – the West of Ireland landscape and Irish identity', in B. O'Connor and M. Cronin (eds.), *Tourism in Ireland: a critical analysis*, Cork University Press, Cork, pp. 86-111.

Nash, C. (1999), 'Landscapes', in P. Cloke, P. Crang and M. Goodwin (eds.), *Introducing human geographies*, Arnold, London, pp. 217-25.

Nash, C. (2000), 'Historical geographies of modernity', in B. Graham and C. Nash (eds.), *Modern historical geographies*, Pearson Education, Essex, pp. 13-40.

Ní Mhainnín, M. and Ó Mhurchú, L. P. (eds.), (1998), *Peig a scéal féin*, An Sagart, An Daingean.

Nöth, W. (1995), *Handbook of semiotics*, Indiana University, Indianapolis.

Nuryanti, W. C. (1996), 'Heritage and postmodern tourism', *Annals of Tourism Research*, Vol. 23 (2), pp. 249-60.

Ó Cinnéide, M. S. (1999), 'Using an area based mark of environmental quality as a means of promoting bottom-up sustainable development', *European Environment*, Vol. 9, pp. 101-8.

Ó Cuív, B. (1968), 'Cath Maige Tuired', in M. Dillon (ed.), *Irish sagas*, Mercier Press, Dublin, pp. 27-39.

O'Connor, B. (1993), 'Myths and mirrors: tourist images and national identity', in B. O'Connor and M. Cronin (eds.), *Tourism in Ireland: a critical analysis*, Cork University Press, Cork, pp. 68-85.

O'Neill, M. A. and Black, M. A. (1996), 'Current quality issues in the Northern Ireland tourism sector', *The Total Quality Magazine*, Vol. 8 (1), pp. 15-19.

O'Neil, P. and Whatmore, S. (2000), 'The business of place: networks of property, partnership and produce', *Geoforum*, Vol. 31, 121-36.

Organisation for Economic Co-operation and Development (1995), *Niche markets as a rural development strategy*, OECD, Paris.

de Paor, L. (1979), 'Ireland's identities', *The Crane Bag*, Vol. 3 (1), pp. 354-61.

Parker, A. J. (1990/1), 'Retail environments: into the 1990s' *Irish marketing review*, Vol. 5 (2), 61-72.

Philo, C. (1993), 'Postmodern rural geography? A reply to Murdoch and Pratt', *Journal of Rural Studies*, Vol. 9 (4), pp. 429-36.

Pickles, J. (1992), 'Texts, hermeneutics and propaganda maps', in T. J. Barnes and J. S. Duncan (eds.), *Writing worlds: discourse, text and metaphor in the representation of landscape*, Routledge, London, pp. 193-230.

Pierce, C. S. (1931-58), *Collected papers*, Harvard University Press, Cambridge.

Poole, M. A. (1997), 'In search of ethnicity in Ireland', in B. Graham (ed.), *In search of Ireland: a cultural geography*, Routledge, London, pp. 128-47.

Poster, M. (1988), *Jean Baudrillard: selected writings*, Polity Press, Cambridge.

Prentice, R. and Andersen, V. (2000), 'Evoking Ireland: modelling tourism propensity', *Annals of Tourism Research*, Vol. 27 (2), pp. 490-516.

Punch, K. F. (1998), *Introduction to social research: quantitative and qualitative approaches*, Sage, London.

Quinn, B. (1994), 'Images of Ireland in Europe: a tourism perspective', in U. Kockel (ed.), *Culture, tourism and development: the case of Ireland*, Liverpool University Press, Liverpool, pp. 61-73.

Quinn, M. (1994), 'Winning service quality-the PROMPT approach', *Irish Marketing Review*, Vol. 7, pp. 110-18.

Ray, C. (1999), 'Endogenous development in the era of reflexive modernity', *Journal of Rural Studies*, Vol. 15 (3), pp. 257-67.

Rigg, J. and Ritchie, M. (2002), 'Production, consumption and imagination in rural Thailand', *Journal of Rural Studies*, Vol. 18 (4), pp. 359-71.

Robertson, R. (1992), *Globalization: social theory and global culture*, Sage London.

Robinson, G. M. (1998), *Methods and techniques in human geography*, Wiley, Chichester.

Rolston, B. (1995), 'Selling tourism in a country at war', *Race and Class*, Vol. 37 (1), pp. 23-40.

Sack, R. (1988), 'The consumer's world: place as context', *Annals of the Association of American Geographers*, Vol. 78 (4), pp. 642-64.

Sack, R. (1992), *Place, modernity and the consumer's world*, The Johns Hopkins University Press, Baltimore.

Said, E. (1993), *Culture and imperialism*, Chatto and Windus, London.

de Saussure, F. (1974), *Course in general linguistics*, Fontana, London.

Schrott, P. R. and Lanoue, D. J. (1994), 'Trends and perspectives in content analysis', in I. Borg and P. Ph. Mohler (eds.), *Trends and perspectives in empirical social research*, Walter de Gruyter, Berlin, pp. 327-45.

Seymour, S. (2000), 'Historical geographies of landscape', in B. Graham and C. Nash (eds.), *Modern historical geographies*, Pearson Education, Essex, pp. 193-217.

Shields, R. (1991), *Places on the margin: alternative geographies of modernity*, Routledge, London.

Sontag, S. (1977), *On photography*, Allen Lane, London.

Spooner, B. (1986), 'Weavers and dealers: the authenticity of an oriental carpet', in A. Appadurai (ed.), *The social life of things: commodities in cultural perspective*, Cambridge University Press, Cambridge, pp. 195-235.

Stake, R. E. (1994), 'Case studies', in N. K. Denzin and Y. S. Lincoln (eds.), *Handbook of qualitative research*, Sage, London, pp. 236-47.

Telfer, D. J. and Wall, G. (1996), 'Linkages between tourism and food production', *Annals of Tourism Research*, Vol. 23 (3), pp. 635-53.

Toal, C. (1995), *North Kerry archaeological survey*, Brandon, Dingle.

Urry, J. (1990), *The tourist gaze*, Routledge, London.

Urry, J. (1995), *Consuming places*, Routledge, London.

Waitt, G. (1997), 'Selling paradise and adventure: representations of landscape in the tourist advertising of Australia', *Australian Geographical Studies*, Vol. 35 (1), pp. 47-60.

Walker, R. (1985a), 'An introduction to applied qualitative research', in R. Walker (ed.), *Applied qualitative research*, Gower, Aldershot, pp. 3-26.

Walker, R. (1985b), 'Evaluating applied qualitative research', in R. Walker (ed.), *Applied qualitative research*, Gower, Aldershot, pp. 177-96.

Walter, J. (1982), 'Social limits to tourism', *Leisure Studies*, Vol. 1, pp. 295-304.

Wang, N. (1999), 'Rethinking authenticity in tourism experience', *Annals of Tourism Research*, Vol. 26 (2), pp. 349-70.

Ward, S. V. (1994), 'Time and place: key themes in place promotion in the USA, Canada and Britain since 1870', in J. R. Gold and S.V. Ward (eds.), *Place promotion: the use of publicity and marketing to sell towns and regions*, Wiley, Chichester, pp. 53-74.

Ward, S. V. (1998), *Selling places: the marketing and promotion of towns and cities 1850-2000*, Routledge, London.

Ward, S.V. and Gold, J. R. (1994), 'Introduction', in J. R. Gold and S. V. Ward (eds.), *Place promotion: the use of publicity and marketing to sell towns and regions*, Wiley, Chichester, pp. 1-17.

Weber, R. P. (1994), 'Basic content analysis', in M. S. Lewis-Beck (ed.), *Research practice*, Sage, London, pp. 251-338.

West Cork LEADER Co-operative Society Ltd. (1998), *Annual report 1997/98*, West Cork LEADER Co-operative Society Ltd., Bandon.

West Cork LEADER Co-operative Society Ltd. (undated), 'West Cork a place apart', a promotional leaflet on the West Cork Fuchsia brand.

Williams, R. (1973), *The country and the city*, Paladin, Hertfordshire.

Willits, F. K. and Luloff, A. E. (1995), 'Urban resident's views of rurality and contacts with rural places', *Rural Sociology*, Vol. 60 (3), pp. 454-66.

Winter, M. (2003), 'Embeddedness, the new food economy and defensive localism', *Journal of Rural Studies*, Vol. 19 (1), pp. 23-32.

Woodward, R. (1996), '"Deprivation" and "the rural": an investigation into contradictory discourses', *Journal of Rural Studies*, Vol. 12 (1), pp. 55-67.

World Tourism Organization (2002), Conclusions of a WTO Seminar on 'Rural tourism in Europe: experiences and perspectives', Belgrade, Yugoslavia, 24-25 June, http://www.world-tourism.org/sustainable/activities/Ruralt-Sem-2002-Concl.pdf.

Yin, R. K. (1998), 'The abridged version of case study research: design and method', in L. Bickman and D. J. Rog (eds.), *Handbook of applied social research methods*, Sage, London, pp. 229-59.

Other Material Cited

Battleship Potemkin (1925), Sergei Eisenstein (Director), Image Entertainment.

Man of Aran (1934), Robert O'Flaherty (Director), Home Vision Entertainment.

The Quiet Man (1952), John Ford (Director), Republic Studios.

Ryan's Daughter (1970), David Lean (Director), Warner Studios.

The Simpsons (1987 – present), Matt Groening (Creator/Executive Producer), Fox Broadcasting Company.

The Untouchables (1987), Brian de Palma (Director), Paramount Studio.

The Naked Gun: From the Files of the Police Squad! (1988), David Zucker (Director), Paramount Studio.

The Naked Gun 2½: The Smell of Fear (1991), David Zucker (Director), Paramount Studio.

The Field (1992), Jim Sheridan (Director), Artisan Entertainment.

The Naked Gun 33⅓: The Final Insult (1994), Peter Segal (Director), Paramount Studio.

Index